Let Your Light Shine
Scripture Stories for Self-Esteem

D0543639

Andre Papineau

LET YOUR LIGHT

SHINE

SCRIPTURE STORIES FOR SELF-ESTEEM

TWENTY-THIRD PUBLICATIONS
Mystic, Connecticut

Scripture selections are taken from the **New American Bible** © 1970 by the Confraternity of Christian Doctrine, Washington, D.C., and are used with permission.

Second printing 1991

Twenty-Third Publications
185 Willow Street
P.O. Box 180
Mystic, CT 06355
(203) 536-2611
800-321-0411

ISBN 0-89622-438-4
Library of Congress Catalog Card Number 90-70561

Dedication

For Dolores Griffin
A light in adversity

Acknowledgment

My special thanks to Dan Pekarske, SDS, for the innumerable hours he has spent editing the material in my books. Without his help and encouragement, I never would have entertained the idea of publishing at all.

CONTENTS

Let Your Light Shine
Scripture Stories for Self-Esteem

INTRODUCTION

Someone says, "Do you know that you can light up everyone's life? Has anyone told you it's as impossible to hide your light as it is to hide the lights of New York, Paris, or London? So let your light shine! Let everybody say, 'Thank God for you who are sparkling from head to foot and warms us up all over!'"

Do we say, "Are you kidding? You don't expect me to believe you, do you? What are you after?" But Jesus says exactly this to us. "You are the light of the world. A city set on a hill cannot be hidden. Men do not light a lamp and then put it under a bushel basket. They set it on a stand where it gives light to all in the house. In the same way, your light must shine before men so that they may see goodness in your acts and give praise to your heavenly Father" (Mt 5:14-16). Yes, it is Jesus who tells us to let our light shine. It is Jesus who proclaims that we have the power to illumine so many lives. And it is Jesus who challenges us to let others see how good we are so that people will say, "Praise God for letting this light shine on us."

Jesus' message is direct, positive, and affirming. Why, then, haven't we taken it to heart? Why do we continue hiding under a basket? Is it because we've been admonished never to be proud, but always to be humble about our gifts and talents? Have we been warned repeatedly, "Don't let it go to your head!" if we seem exuberant about some accomplishment like getting top honors in school, giving a bravura performance on the piano, scoring the winning touchdown?

Having been cautioned, chastised, or corrected for beaming over our achievements, we've either felt obliged to revel secretly or to minimize or deny our accomplishments. We learned to act cool and dispassionate so that we wouldn't appear arrogant. "Oh, it was nothing," or "It wasn't that good," or "Others have done much better than I" are some of our stock responses to praise. To say "I really did a good job," or "I think I really shone tonight" might seem worse to us than spouting obscenities!

Unfortunately, some of us have dismissed any and everything we've accomplished in life as worthless. From a very early age we learned to minimize and devalue whatever we'd done. If we brought home four A's and a B on a report card, our parents might have said, "What? Why didn't you get all A's?" "Never enough" is the message many of us received regarding our achievements in the classroom, on the athletic field, in the arts, etc., so that now we never believe our light shines enough—or shines at all.

Why do such common childhood hurts seem to have such tragic consequences in adult life? The late Heinz Kohut, a psychiatrist who founded Self Psychology, studied how a child acquires a sense of self-worth. He theorized that infants depend on two external sources for developing some sense of who they are: a "mirroring other" and an "idealized other." The "mirroring other" reflects back to the infant the infant's sense of greatness. We might call this the "wow" effect. The "Wow, you're great!" in the mother's oohs and aahs becomes the child's "Wow, I'm great!" It is the precursor of "self-wowing," that is, of self-admiration, or the recognition of one's own light. Inadequate mirroring during childhood produces an adult forever looking to others for the self-validation missed as a child.

In addition to the "mirroring other," children depend on an "ideal other." This other represents the light greater than oneself. Often the father seems to be an all-powerful other whom the child esteems, admires, and looks up to, and with whose strength the child needs to merge. In this process the other's strength and light temporarily become the child's. Gradually, the external, idealized parent is transformed into the child's own internal ideals and aspirations. This, in turn, inspires and guides the child into maturity. Lacking an idealized other, the child grows up to become a person whose importance is dependent upon being attached to idealized others, external lights, e.g., rock stars, gurus, politicians, actors, etc.

Assimilating both the "idealized other" and the "mirroring other" is what ultimately constitutes one's own basic self. Only children who accomplish this can grow to provide for themselves what initially only the parents could provide. If there is no one available either to mirror or to be an ideal for the child, the result is a light "hidden" under a basket.

This book affirms and re-echoes Jesus' challenge to us that we let our light shine. As participants in the Light, we have the potential, or God power, to illumine our world and to bring the Light of Life to others, each in our unique way. How are we unique embodiments of the Light?

Simply consider some of the many different kinds of people we experience and how their lights have affected us. Like porchlights lit for visitors, some people are welcoming presences in our lives, while others guide us unobtrusively along like hallway nightlights. We are inspired by visionaries who shine like stars and we are cheered by those who afford the steady flame of the candle. And every now and then a person enters our life like a meteor shooting through the heavens. Some personalities are flashy like neon lights; others are as brilliant as the noonday sun; still others are penetrating lasers or searching floodlights.

We can imagine ourselves as any of these kinds of lights at various times in our lives. At one point we need to be aspiring stars and at other times we serve as footlights for others. Sometimes we shine brilliantly; at other times we are more subdued. Whatever our light, it is always light from Light and not the Light itself. Only when we are mindful of this truth can we welcome the different epiphanies of light into our lives. Circumscribed as we are by darkness, we always stand in need of others' light to illumine our ignorance and blindness so that we may participate even more fully in the "true light that enlightens everyone" (Jn 1:9).

I hope the stories in this book will help you to understand why we hide under baskets and what steps we need to take to let our light shine. Perhaps, as you read these stories and reflections, you may begin to feel your light burning more intensely. If that happens, we have already taken the first crucial step in letting our light shine more brightly.

LINE DRAWING

*On one occasion a lawyer stood up and posed him this problem:
"Teacher, what must I do to inherit everlasting life?" Jesus answered him: "What is written in the law? How do you read it?" He
replied:*

"You shall love the Lord your God
with all your heart,
with all your soul, with all your strength,
and with all your mind;
and your neighbor as yourself."

*Jesus said, "You have answered correctly. Do this and you shall
live." But because he wished to justify himself he said to Jesus, "And
who is my neighbor?" Luke 10:25-37*

"Where do you draw the line?" Abe demanded. "When is
enough enough? Just how far do I have to go?" Abe was a
lawyer who felt compelled to know exactly what the law stip-
ulated for every issue imaginable. "It's my training," he explained to a friend. "We lawyers are expected to spell out others' rights and responsibilities under the law. We aren't hired
to give fuzzy answers. No, sir! Our clients demand precision!"

But Abe needed precision not only for his clients. He had
endless questions about his own obligations. "When I go
strolling in the park, how many times should I tip my hat to a
person I've passed three times in the same day? When someone wants to borrow money, how much do I have to lend

5

them before I say 'Enough is enough'? How much time must I spend with a friend filling me in on all his little problems? The same for my relatives? Just where do I draw the line?"

He consulted other lawyers. He searched and researched dust-covered tomes and scholarly periodicals for answers. And when he'd light upon one, Abe was noticeably relieved. "Ahh! If I meet someone three times a day, I tip my hat once, nod a second time, and wave a third." Or, "I lend twenty per cent of a day's wage to my friend, thirty per cent to my first cousin, forty per cent to my brother, fifty per cent to my wife, and seventy-five per cent to my mother. At that point, enough is enough! Good, now I know!" Or, "Depending on how long I've known the friend, the time I must spend listening ranges from five minutes for a new acquaintance to an hour and a half for a grade school chum. Then I can draw the line and say 'Enough is enough'."

True, Abe might be inconvenienced by what the law required, but inconveniences didn't matter nearly as much as knowing clearly what was expected. For example, if a friend deserved an hour's hearing, according to the law, whether he droned on about trivia or desperately needed Abe's attention, Abe had to listen. Only after the full hour was up could he say, "Well, enough is enough. I draw the line here." Then could he dismiss the friend whether the friend continued to need him or not.

Needless to say, this need to know exactly what was expected of him came to be the source of much consternation. One day as he walked down a deserted street Abe spied a man, bruised and beaten, lying in a gutter. The man was black, dressed in a white suit, black shirt, and purple tie. He was barely conscious. His panama hat and cane, broken sunglasses, and empty wallet lay scattered about the sidewalk. Abe was shocked as he approached, but stopped short. "I know him! My God, what am I going to do? It's the pimp from K Street! We've been trying to clean up his neighborhood for years. If it weren't for him and his stable of hookers, we'd have no problems! Hmmmm, he's bleeding badly. Maybe one of *them* clobbered him. Serves him right! But do I have to help him? Him, of all people? A pimp? The law—what does it say about helping wounded pimps? How far do I have to go? Where do I draw the line? When can I say enough is enough?"

Abe was in such a quandary that he simply wandered off without helping the man, leaving him to an uncertain fate. For the next couple of days Abe did what he always did in these situations. He searched and researched the tomes, and consulted his lawyer friends. However, he got no satisfactory answers about whether the law demanded helping pimps. Walking home from his club, still agonizing over what was expected of him, he came across a small crowd of people listening to an itinerant preacher. "It's Jesus," he muttered. "I've heard him before. Good speaker! I wonder..." Abe stood listening. When Jesus had finished speaking, Abe blurted out, much to his own surprise, "Teacher, what must I do to inherit everlasting life?"

Jesus shaded his eyes, looked long and hard at Abe, and asked, "What is written in the law? How do you read it?"

Abe was relieved. He knew the law on that one. "You shall love the Lord your God with all your heart, with all your soul, with all your strength, and with all your mind, and your neighbor as yourself."

Jesus said "You have answered correctly. Do this and you shall live." But Abe wouldn't drop the matter. That law wasn't clear enough. He needed to know exactly where to draw the line. "Who...who is my neighbor?"

Jesus answered, "There was a man about your size, wearing a blue suit and gold-rimmed glasses like yours, carrying your kind of brown briefcase, on his way from Jerusalem to Jericho. Waiting in the bushes alongside the road were three robbers. They jumped him, beat him, took his money, and then left him for dead.

"An hour passed and a man dressed in a blue suit and

wearing gold-rimmed glasses like yours came down the road. He also happened to be carrying a brown briefcase. When he saw the man, he stopped, opened his briefcase and removed a book called *Line Drawing*. Thumbing through it, he reached a certain page, read it, nodded confidently, closed the book, put it back into his case, and walked on.

"Half an hour later another man looking surprisingly like you came down the road, saw the man, halted, and produced a scholarly book from his briefcase. It was titled *When Enough Is Enough*. Thumbing through it several times, checking and rechecking the index and appendices, he frowned, fidgeted, and sighed. He paced up and down the road for twenty minutes deep in thought. Then, shrugging his shoulders, he walked on.

"Finally, another man came down the road. He wore a white suit, black shirt, purple tie, panama hat, sunglasses, and carried a cane. He was black. He was also the town pimp. Seeing the injured man, he ran over to him, knelt down and exclaimed, 'What can I do for you my man?' He took a small flask of whiskey from his suit pocket, gave the injured man a drink, got him to his feet, and practically carried him to a motel a mile down the road. There the pimp told the innkeeper, 'Watch out for my man here. I'll pay you when I come back.'

"Now I ask you, which of these three proved to be a neighbor?"

Abe was dumbfounded. "Well, not the one who consulted *Line Drawing*."

"Yes. Go on."

"And...uh...not the other fella who relied on *When Enough Is Enough*."

"Who was it, then?" Jesus insisted.

"The p...p...p...pimp," Abe sputtered.

Jesus winked. "Then go and do likewise. Enough line drawing, OK?"

"Yeah, sure, no line drawing," Abe answered. He had learned that enough is never enough.

REFLECTION

"Where do I draw the line?" is not an entirely selfish question. It is an acknowledgment that we are limited in what we can and cannot do. As humans we are finite. When we constantly overextend ourselves, we are playing at being God. We need limits. However, the honest admission that we have to draw the line ought not to be turned into our life's theme.

"Where do I draw the line" as a life theme becomes a self-imposed limitation not only on what I have to be in relation to others but also on what I can become. Our concern to do only what is required blinds us to our own potential for becoming all that we can become in a variety of relationships. In terms of letting our light shine, we don't want to limit the light by asking how much we have to shine. Rather we want to realize whatever our possibilities are for shining.

If our life theme is "Where do I draw the line?" we might ask ourselves why we insist on drawing lines at all. Do we fear losing ourselves in too much caring and too much giving? Whatever the reason for our fear, only taking the step of trust in the Unbounded Light will really let us shine. Only that will enable us to say enough is never enough!

THE LAST LAUGH

Now Abraham and Sarah were old, advanced in years, and Sarah had stopped having her womanly periods. So Sarah laughed to herself and said, "Now that I am so withered and my husband is so old, am I still to have sexual pleasure?" But the LORD said to Abraham, "Why did Sarah laugh and say, 'Shall I really bear a child, old as I am?' Is anything too marvelous for the LORD to do?"

Genesis 18:11-14

"Sarah, the drought has dwindled our food supply. There are difficult times ahead but we'll survive," her mother assured her.

"Ha! Ha! Ha!" Sarah laughed until her belly ached—or did she laugh because it ached?

"Sarah, you have all the qualifications: intelligence, personality, character references. There's only one hitch. Your skin's too dark! Sorry, we'll have to hire someone else for the position," the amiable manager smiled as he walked her to the door.

"Ha! Ha! Ha!" Sarah clenched her teeth, bit her lip, and laughed her hurt away.

"Sarah, a woman belongs to her husband. She's not supposed to think for herself. And why would you want to anyway? To prove you're better than a man?" her teacher reproved her.

Sarah rapped her fingers on the desk, sailed a sigh through the air, and trailed it with laughter. "Ha! Ha! Ha!"

Sarah's response to adversity was unusual. Unlike others who cried, perspired, swore, got angry, developed migraines or ulcers, broke out in hives or cold sweat, Sarah laughed. She couldn't tell you why she laughed but one thing she knew, her laughter kept her going through thick and thin. Yes, she laughed whether she wanted to or not. It was a mixed blessing.

The same laughter that often helped relieve tension frequently created even more. For example, in the early days of married life friction flared between Abe and Sarah because Abe misunderstood her laughter.

Masking the fear in her eyes, Sarah giggled uncontrollably when Abe said the Lord God commanded them to leave the security of home and country for a new land they had never seen or even heard of. "Ha! Ha! Ha!"

"I don't think it's one bit funny! We're going to a distant country, not our neighbor's tent! We need faith and lots of it, not this silly giggling," he lectured her. But his serious tone simply deepened the tension.

"Ha! Ha! Ha! Oops!" Sarah blurted, bringing both hands to her mouth in a vain attempt to stifle her laughter. Understandably, Abe was smarting as he stormed away wondering who the woman was he had married.

But there were other times when Sarah's laughter served them well, like the time she and Abe traveled to Egypt. There had been a famine in Canaan but plenty of food in Egypt. However, while they solved one problem by going to Egypt, they came up against another once they arrived. Sarah's good looks had drawn the attention of the Pharaoh. Fearful he would lose his life if the Pharaoh discovered Sarah was his wife, Abe introduced her to the Egyptian court as his sister. Neither Sarah nor Abe knew whether the members of the court would believe their story. Naturally, Sarah was extremely nervous. But Abe had told her, "Just have faith and everything will be OK! We'll be able to stay here in Egypt."

"Most pleased to meet you, madam. You are beautiful indeed."

"Ha! Ha! Ha!" Tittering, Sarah blushed brightly.

"What do you think of our country?" he queried.

"Ha! Ha! Ha!" Sarah struggled and sputtered but couldn't speak.

Nevertheless, the courtiers were captivated.

"And your laughter lightens our lives," chortled the others.

"Ha! Ha! Ha!" Surprise! Sarah's laughter impressed the court and saved the day. Or did it? She was such a hit that Sarah was "invited" to Pharaoh's chambers for the night.

Knocking warily on the chamber door that evening, she wondered what she'd do and how she'd act. "Ha! Ha! Ha!" Beside herself with fear, she laughed uncontrollably as Pharaoh greeted her with open arms.

"You're every bit the beauty they say you are," Pharaoh marveled as he drew her to his bed. "By the way, since you laugh so easily I have a joke or two for you," he winked as he sat her next to him.

Wide-eyed, Sarah broke out into paroxysms of laughter whenever Pharaoh delivered his royal punch lines. "Ha! Ha! Ha!" He was delighted that Sarah laughed at jokes even he hadn't thought funny, much less the members of the royal household.

"Now enough of mirth. Let's to bed, my love," he whispered sweetly in her ear. As Pharaoh disrobed, Sarah doubled over with fits of laughter.

"Ha! Ha! Ha! Ha! Ha! Ha!"

"Is it something about my body that strikes you funny?" he asked defensively.

"Ha! Ha! Ha!" Sarah squirmed, stuffing the corner of the pillow into her mouth. His face crimson with anger, the Pharaoh scrambled for a sheet, wrapped it around himself and ordered her out of the chamber. "Ha! Ha! Ha!" Tears streaming down her cheeks, Sarah sailed home on waves of laughter. No sooner had she arrived than Pharaoh's word overtook her and Abe.

"Out! Out! Out of my country!"

"Tsk! Tsk! Tsk! Not enough faith, Sarah. That's why we've failed," Abe muttered as they left Pharaoh's land.

Back in Canaan, her troubles continued. Abe was particularly disturbed by her laughing whenever he built altars at wayside shrines. He took his relationship with God very seriously. No one was permitted a word while he meticulously piled up the stones, and everyone was to stay completely silent whenever he performed the sacrifice. Of course in such a super-charged atmosphere, it was inevitable that Sarah would laugh.

"Ha! Ha! Ha!" she laughed one day as Abe was bowing profoundly at a wayside shrine. "Ha! Ha! Ha!"

Arching an eyebrow, Abe exploded. "Laughing during a service at a shrine! You've actually laughed! Don't you realize believing is no laughing matter? Faith and foolishness don't mix," he decreed. "What kind of a God do you think we follow anyway?"

"Ha! Ha! Ha! Surely not a God who cannot laugh," she bristled. The other members of the party weren't quite certain what to make of all this, but they secretly agreed among themselves that laughter was preferable to the unrelieved seriousness and boredom that marked Abe's worship.

Sarah's inability to conceive occasioned more bouts of laughter than anything else in her life. "Ha! Ha! Ha! I can't bear a child," she moaned. "Ha! Ha! Ha! Abe, take my servant girl Hagar and have a child by her. Ha! Ha! Ha!" Now, she suffered the double indignity of not being able to conceive and of turning to her servant for help.

She laughed through it all in spite of her tears, a response some of her friends believed helped Sarah maintain her sanity. "Ha! Ha! Ha!" Her laughter was tinged with defiance when Hagar took advantage of her pregnancy and frequently insulted Sarah.

As Sarah grew old and wrinkled, she continued to laugh in the face of difficulties that might have caused men and women half her age to weep. Getting up in the morning she'd feel arthritis aching in her hands and legs. "Ha! Ha! Ha!" She winced, but still the laughter rose to heaven. And when she'd sit and consider how she'd fare when she could no longer see or hear, she'd throw her hands up in desperation and then break into a laugh undiminished by her years. "Ha! Ha! Ha!"

One day three strangers paid Abe a visit while he stood fanning himself at the entrance to his tent. Being a hospitable man, he invited them to stay for a snack. They accepted and sat on a blanket in the shade of a nearby tree. While they got settled, Abe whispered in the tent for Sarah to bake some tea rolls for them. Then he joined his guests. After they had eaten, one of the guests dropped a bombshell. "About this time next year I'll return and when I do Sarah will have a child."

Sarah who had been eavesdroping at the entrance of the tent began to laugh. "Ha! Ha! Ha!" She couldn't stop. "After all these years, Abe at 100: no teeth, can hardly walk, barely sees and as far as I know...Ha! Ha! Ha! And me at 90? Ha! Ha! Ha! What's Abe been giving them to drink? Ha! Ha! Ha! And the baby will be here next year? Ha! Ha! Ha!"

What Sarah didn't realize, though Abe did, was that the stranger who spoke was the Lord God. After all, who else could have made such a promise? "There is nothing the Lord can't do!" Abe thundered in anger and exasperation. "After all these years don't you have faith? I know...it takes a lot of effort to believe but with enough willpower you can do it! You..."

"Why were you laughing, Sarah?" the Lord God interrupted.

"I wasn't laughing," she said. "Ha! Ha! Ha! It's just that I...Abe...me...we....mommy and daddy...Ha! Ha! Ha! It's wonderful!"

The Lord God could not reprimand Sarah. He remembered her history, how Sarah's laughter had gotten her this far in life. And he wasn't about to chastise her for the one thing that would have to get her through the rest. He, too, smiled at the thought of how old Abe and Sarah would be when they became the proud parents of their firstborn. "Ha! Ha!" he laughed. "Abe, you've got to admit, it is funny when you come to think of it."

Abe looked dumbly at the Lord God. "Am I missing the point of something?" he wondered.

And that day the Lord God thought he'd had the last laugh. He didn't. The following year, as God had promised, she had her baby. And they named the baby Isaac, which means he laughs!

REFLECTION

Some people come out from under the basket in times of adversity. It is then that their light really shines. We read of people who lose homes and possessions in earthquakes, tornadoes, or hurricanes rising to the occasion and rebuilding their lives. Or we read of a college student standing his ground against a column of tanks rolling ominously towards him on a Beijing street. Or on our televisions we see ordinary people marching to protest the presence of crack houses in the inner cities. True, the protests may appear puny considering the opposition. After all, what does the student accomplish in barring the way of tanks; what do marchers achieve in raising their voices against an immense drug problem?

But some people insist on coming out of hiding and letting their lights shine. Intimidation intensifies rather than diminishes many persons' desire to be heard and seen. In *Last Laugh*, Sarah's laughter is the light that breaks through adversity. During her life so many people mistook her laughter for everything but what it was, i.e., a light which could not be overcome by any of the injustices to which she was subjected. Even Abe, the man of faith, failed to appreciate his wife's growing faith as she laughed her way through one trial after another. If laughter is the best medicine, it is also frequently the best way to let our light shine in the presence of adversity.

When have we experienced hardships which have intensified, instead of diminished, the light?

WHO'S DESERVING?

But the LORD sent a large fish, that swallowed Jonah and he remained in the belly of the fish three days and three nights. Jonah 3:1

"I'll never go fishing again," Jonah promised as he straggled onto the deserted shore of Nineveh's Sin City Beach. "I've smelled enough fish in three days to last for a lifetime. And I suppose I'm the only one who knows a fish inside and out," he sniffed.

Three days earlier, while he had floated in the cavernous belly of the whale, Jonah had all but despaired of ever seeing the light of day again. Fortunately, the Lord must have dropped some very potent pepper in the whale's spout, because it had sneezed so hard Jonah flew out of the whale and into the shallow waters of the beach.

Having caught his breath, Jonah stumbled no more than a couple of yards when he spied a message written on the sand that reminded him how he had gotten into his predicament in the first place. The message was brief. "Go to Nineveh and announce to it the message I will tell you." He scrutinized the handwriting and muttered, "Yeah, it's his all right! What choice do I have?" The handwriting was there for Jonah to see and he couldn't avoid it.

Nor had he been unable to avoid it the first time he saw it spraypainted across his front door back home. That message was also brief. "Set out for the great city of Nineveh and preach against it; their wickedness has come up before me." Jonah needed no one then to tell him that the Lord was responsible for that order. The peculiar slant to the letters and the uncrossed t's helped him decide they were the Lord's words. It was common knowledge that that was how the Lord's penmanship appeared on the tablets Moses had gotten from the Lord on Sinai. But what really convinced Jonah that the Lord was responsible for the graffiti on his door was the paint itself. "It's so luminous! We don't have paint that glows like that around here," he marveled.

Jonah, however, wasn't happy about having to make the trip. He suspected that the Lord would change his mind and spare the Ninevites once Jonah got there. "He likes to come off as being the tough guy but he's a marshmallow. All anyone needs to do is shed a tear and he breaks down," Jonah told a friend. "Well, I don't want to bring these people the bad news unless it stays bad news. Those Ninevites are a sick lot and they deserve to be punished! So I'll be darned if I'm going all that distance to have the Lord go easy on them." Having given the matter serious thought, he decided to vacation in sunny southern Tarshish until the Lord reconsidered sending him to Nineveh.

What Jonah hadn't expected and soon discovered was how well the Lord could play the heavy. Violent storms threatened to destroy the boat on which he was bound for Tarshish. The other passengers and crew investigated and concluded Jonah was responsible. Reluctant as they were to throw him overboard, Jonah urged them to do so. "Look, I'm already retching terribly from seasickness. I might as well be dead." So they threw him overboard. But, as luck would have it, a whale was in the neighborhood and just happened to be yawning when Jonah sailed right into its mouth. One gulp and Jonah's vacation plans had gone into a three-day hold!

Now, however, as he read and reread the message on the sandy beach, he realized he had to do the Lord's bidding. Shaking his head in the direction of Nineveh, he said, "Such a city. It's too big and the plumbing is bad. I hear the people hardly ever bathe. Phew! And it's so hot this time of the year. Oy vey! I can smell it already. Why wasn't I sent in winter?" There was no answer.

Resigned to his fate, Jonah began his journey to Nineveh. He had painted black letters on a white sandwich board which announced the destruction of Nineveh in forty days. Wearing the sign, he marched down the streets shouting, "Nineveh's had it! It's all over, folks! In forty days the city will be torched. Too bad! You deserve what's coming!" Jonah seemed to relish the message of gloom and doom. Smiling broadly, he preached over and over that they deserved to be punished, and whenever he got a whiff of a particularly smelly citizen, he held his nose and added, "For that alone you deserve punishment!" But punishment was not to be the order of the day.

Jonah hadn't even put in a full day's work when he came across men and women everywhere who were painting messages in black letters on white sandwich boards as he had done....but with an entirely different message. "Sorry, God. We've been schlmiels. Forgive us. It's sackcloth and ashes time!"

Flailing his arms and hands, Jonah protested. "No! You can't do that! What right do you have to be sorry? You've had your fling and gotten your fun. Now you deserve to pay for it! No getting off scot free! No siree! Once down, always down, I say. There's no way back up!"

But still more and more people, as well as cats and dogs, wore the sandwich boards so that the city resembled an island of waddling penguins. And on a marquee overlooking the Palace Theater in the middle of Nineveh a neon light flashed on and off. "Repent and be saved! Tomorrow's apparel: Sackcloth and ashes. Signed: The King and I."

Shaking his fist at the sign, Jonah was furious. Still, his fury wasn't nearly as great as his frustration when he happened to look up into the heavens and saw skywriting which read, "All is forgiven. I love you all." Jonah tore off his sandwich board, threw it on the ground, jumped up and down on it several times, and chanted "Damn! Damn! Damn! I knew you'd be a marshmallow, Lord. Not toward me, of course. Oh, no! Me you pursued like the furies! I've had it! I've had it! I've had it, Lord! Life is not worth living when there is so much forgiveness in the land. Let me die!" As he stomped on the sandwich board he couldn't help noticing familiar scribbling in chalk on the concrete walk. "Why so angry?" it read.

"Ohhh!" Jonah groaned and marched angrily out of the city. When he had gotten to the outskirts he bought a pup tent, set it up, and wailed, "Maybe the Lord will see the error of his ways and repent of the mercy he intends to show these people. I'll wait and see." He stationed himself at the front of his tent in the noonday sun and, much to his surprise, a small plant shot up through the soil and grew until it was ten feet tall. It then sprouted branches and leaves that afforded shade and refreshed Jonah. "Gee, I didn't even plant the seed," he exclaimed. "What did I do to deserve this?" Then he fell into a deep sleep.

The next morning as he lay half asleep under the tree, he thought he heard a strange sound. Chomp, chomp, chomp! Opening his eyes, he was horrified. There were ten huge worms greedily devouring the leaves on the branches. "Oh, no!" he cried. Within minutes the leaves were eaten. Once more he was exposed to the hot sun and burning wind. "What did I do to deserve this? I want to die," he complained. As he turned to go into his pup tent he was startled to see a message spraypainted across the front of it. The penmanship and the paint were unmistakably the Lord's. And the message? "So who says *deserves* has anything to do with anything? Easy come, easy go!"

Jonah scratched his head and pondered the message. He

hadn't deserved the shade tree nor had he deserved its removal. Deserve had nothing to do with it! Slowly he looked to the city of Nineveh. "Deserve has nothing to do with what's happening today," he whispered. "Nothing at all!" Again he stood for several seconds and then smiled. Picking up his sandals, he walked to the side of the tent and...another message! "Don't worry; be happy!" it said. Jonah decided that if he were happy, it wasn't because he deserved it. Shrugging his shoulders, he looked up into the sky and laughed, "Easy come, easy go!"

REFLECTION

When we catch a fish we have him on the hook. If the fish is too small or if we have one fish too many, we take it off the hook and throw it back.

Many of us play the hook game with other people. We catch people when they say something self-incriminating. "Don't lie to me! I spoke to seven people who saw you there!" Or we catch them in the act and say, "Didn't I tell you—no cookies before dinner!" We catch them cheating, making love, making faces, etc. And once we catch them we seldom act as kindly toward them as we do toward fish. "Let them wriggle," we say. We're not going to let them off the hook. No way! They deserve to suffer for what they've done. And if someone says, "I'm sorry," or "I won't do it again," we're still not going to let them off the hook that easily. "Not so fast, Buster. You've got a lot of explaining to do," or "It doesn't work that way—you can't act as though nothing's happened!" Even if the person acknowledges hurting us and wants to make amends, we aren't going to let the sucker off the hook! We've got him right where we want him and we intend to keep him there.

Are we very different from Jonah after all? We think that people deserve what they get. Jonah's attitude contrasts sharply with God's who, in Jonah's estimation, is a marshmallow when it comes to letting people off the hook. Don't we often share that attitude? What would become of people if we let them off the hook? How would they act if we didn't let them know that we possessed the power to let them off the hook? Or if we failed to remind them daily who had let them go free? Or that they'd be on the hook again if they tried something silly?

We shudder to think what using God's gentle approach to forgiveness might release on the world! That God's light should shine on the bad as well as the good doesn't make sense to us.

Yet God's light, like the sun's, shines on all. If we are participating in God's light, then aren't we "cheating" God by letting our light shine on some and withholding it from others? Do we need to step out into the sun and remind ourselves that the sun has been there for us whether we've deserved it or not?

SHORT ON MEMORY

Then Peter came up and asked him, "Lord, when my brother wrongs me, how often must I forgive him? Seven times?" "No," Jesus replied, "not seven times; I say, seventy times seven times. That is why the reign of God may be said to be like a king who decided to settle accounts with his officials. When he began his auditing, one was brought in who owed him a huge amount." Matthew 18:21-24

The king was furious. "I want him thrown into prison—him and his whole family!" All of his advisors agreed. Ben had betrayed the king's trust and he deserved to be severely punished. Ben had been hired three years earlier through his father's intercession. The older man had himself been a trusted advisor to the king.

"You've been very loyal to me," the king had told Ben's father. "How could I forget your loyalty? I'd be ungrateful if I denied your request." Ben was elated when he got the news of his appointment as the king's valet. Gradually he ingratiated himself through his wit and disarming manner. As valet, Ben frequently had occasion to be alone with the king. He welcomed these occasions to find out as discreetly as possible what was going on in the king's personal life. Consequently, he listened attentively to every word the king spoke and, as time passed, the king was deeply moved by this attention.

"We need men like you," the king commended him one

day. And from that point on the king confided everything in him. It was highly unusual for a sovereign to place such trust in a commoner but the king was extraordinarily good to Ben. Strolling together in the palace halls or the royal gardens, dining privately with the king for lunch, and horseback riding with him in the early morning hours, Ben gave an ear to all the king's problems with his wife and children, regarding his deepest fears about himself, concerning the future of the kingdom. "I don't think of you as an advisor, Ben. I consider you my friend; I'm able to tell you secrets I don't even share with the queen."

"Thank you, majesty. I'm grateful to you for thinking of me as your friend. I would never betray a confidence. Your trust hasn't been misplaced." But what the king didn't know was that Ben was actually disclosing the nature of these private chats to whoever paid the highest price. He received large sums of money from those who needed information either to promote their own careers or to subvert the king's policies. Ben was very discreet in his disclosures at first, but as time went on, he felt more and more invincible and he grew reckless in his speech.

Then one day he bragged to an ambassador, "The king has planned a secret attack against your northern border and I can give you the details." He told him the time and place of the attack, the number of forces the king intended to use, and the king's strategy for winning the battle. What he didn't know was that the foreign official was secretly loyal to the king, and within an hour Ben was hauled into the royal courtroom.

Yes, the king's reaction was to get revenge and have him thrown into prison. Angered and deeply hurt, he cried, "How could you have done this to me?"

Terrified at the prospect of going to prison, Ben prostrated himself at the king's feet. "Majesty, I beg you, reconsider! Think of the good times we've enjoyed together. Surely your memory is not so short that you have forgotten?"

The king shook his head sadly and turned the question

back on Ben. "Have you forgotten how I took you in when you had no work? Don't you remember dining at my table and drinking my wine?" Ben was silent. "I want you and your family thrown..." The king paused for a moment...then whispered, "Wait!" Closing his eyes, he said softly, "Ah, yes, I remember." But what the king remembered had nothing to do with Ben.

He remembered a day long ago when, as a young prince, he had betrayed his own father, the old king, all because of some slight he thought he had received from him. He recalled foolishly gathering other young hotheads in the realm to plan a coup against his father. However, having gotten wind of the plot, his father simply reprimanded the prince and the others. He refused to hold anything against them. Rather he chalked the whole incident up to youthful folly. Remembering how overwhelmed he was by his father's mercy, the king realized that never until this minute had he been able to do for anyone else what his father had done for him. Saddened as he was by Ben's betrayal, the memory of his father's mercy prompted him to leniency. "I will not hold this against you or your family. You are free to leave."

"Thank you, thank you. I am most grateful to you," Ben blurted as he got to his knees before the king. Tears flowing down his cheeks, he cried, "I do not know how to thank you!"

"Just remember!" the king advised.

"Remember? Yes, yes," Ben agreed even though he really didn't understand what the king meant. What mattered most to him was that he was free. Rising to his feet, Ben left the royal courtroom.

No longer in the service of the king, Ben had to find other means of employment. Since he was short on funds, he decided to visit a friend to whom he had lent a small amount of money two years earlier. "I need my money now," he demanded.

"But I can't pay you now; I barely have enough money to support myself and my family."

"I don't care about your family. I need it now! And if I don't get it—then you can spend some time in prison."

Horrified, his friend pleaded, "Ben, remember the good times we've had together! Is this the way you treat your friends?"

But Ben was short on memory. Not only had he had a memory lapse regarding the good times they had together, but he had forgotten the pardon the king had granted him. And having forgotten, he had no grateful heart to prompt him to forgive his friend. "It's off to prison, then, for you."

When news of what Ben had done reached the king, he was extremely angry. "How little Ben remembers," he thought. Once more he was tempted to throw Ben into prison. But again he remembered how gracious his own father had been toward him, and again he changed his mind. "I cannot be ungrateful," he said. So the king ordered the release of the friend to whom Ben had lent the money.

"What about Ben?" the advisors asked. "Surely you are going to punish him?"

"No," the king answered. "He's short on memory and since he can't remember, he's locked out of his heart as well. Prison can't be worse than that!"

The counselors agreed. To be short on memory is indeed a curse worse than prison itself. And so it was that Ben roamed the countryside suffering from the disease called short on memory.

REFLECTION

The German philosopher Martin Heidegger said that thinking is thanking. In a less philosophical vein, Bob Hope sings "Thanks for the Memories." Remembering and thanking are closely related. Their connection is especially clear when we go to someone's wake. There we gather and share stories about our dead friend or loved one. Through these anecdotes and stories we become grateful that this person touched our lives. And being grateful can motivate us to be a bit more gracious toward others as the deceased had been toward us. If we are short on memory, however, thankfulness eludes us as well and we are seldom moved to be gracious toward others.

Our story about Ben illustrates the tragedy of not remembering another's gracious actions in our lives. In this case failure to remember moments of forgiveness with gratitude inhibits the servant from being forgiving to others. How often when we forgive do we remind others of how indebted they are to us for that very forgiveness? Beneficiaries of this kind of forgiveness stand to lose more than gain. Forgiveness given grudgingly makes us feel the weight of guilt more intensely, whereas we feel relief if it is given graciously.

Can we remember the people who have been gracious to us? Can that in turn help us become more gracious in our own lives? When we remember will we also become people of light like the young king in the story?

RISEN

He offered them still another image: "The reign of God is like yeast which a woman took and kneaded into three measures of flour. Eventually the whole mass of dough began to rise." Matthew 13:33

Her friends called her Prissy. On occasion, they affectionately referred to her as "Miss Prim and Proper Prissy." Priscilla Prudell didn't mind being called Prissy by her friends in her home or in theirs, but she insisted it was only proper she be called Priscilla in public. "It's Priscilla," she admonished others in supermarkets, department stores, sidewalk cafes, and even on empty streets.

Not only was Priscilla very proper about the use of her name, she was also always properly preened. Her hair tightly drawn back into a bun, she wore modest dresses which never accented her shape in any way that might attract the least attention to herself. And she always had the scent of Ivory soap about her because she bathed twice a day to keep herself as clean as she could be.

Priscilla was also properly punctual. If she said she'd meet someone at 7:00 P.M., then she'd be at the appointed place at seven sharp. Or if she invited a friend to dinner for 8:00 P.M., the friend knew if she came one half hour late, she could expect to be on time for dessert and nothing more. Everything at the proper time and in the proper place was the way Priscilla played out her life.

She even prayed properly. No outbursts of passion in her prayers! Never did she dialogue with the deity in any easy manner. God forbid! Priscilla demonstrated her deference to the Lord of Order and Restraint by crafting her words into a careful colloquy. She simply never used words like "hell" and "damn." She never even entertained employing such words when she addressed the Divine...or anyone else for that matter.

No wonder her friends referred to her as prim and proper. Still they loved her—for her good works, her sincerity, and her fidelity to them in times of need. But most especially they loved her for what she termed her "lapses in decorum." These were the unguarded moments when she'd begin to giggle or cry or get angry in spite of herself. Her friends noted affectionately how free she was during these times. Invariably, however, Priscilla apologized profusely for her aberrant behavior. "Oh, this isn't like me. I'll see it doesn't happen again." Her friends hoped that one day Priscilla Prudell would surrender some of her propriety for everybody's sake, including her own. And what they hoped for happened in a most peculiar way.

Priscilla had invited two of her friends over for a Tuesday evening dinner. She had decided to bake raisin bread for the dinner on the night before the soirée. So she marshaled all the ingredients on the kitchen counter and methodically set about mixing flour, salt and sugar, melting butter, readying the yeast, and setting aside raisins from a cardboard container. After mixing the ingredients, she thoroughly kneaded the dough until it looked the picture of perfection. "Very good," she said. "I'll give it an hour to rise. One hour," she addressed the lump of dough as she set it aside and covered it with a towel.

Exactly an hour later she returned. The dough hadn't risen—at all! Priscilla pursed her lips, swallowed hard, rapped her fingers on the counter and whispered very softly, "One more hour...do you hear?"

Yet another hour passed. She returned punctually. Still the dough hadn't risen, not even so much as an inch! Priscilla's face reddened. She glared at the lifeless dough. Carefully rolling up her sleeves and smoothing any wayward curls, she muttered between her teeth, "OK, OK, it's one hour more for you and then," she nodded ominously towards the wastebasket. "Get my point?"

A third time she returned. But not at the hour she had set for herself. No. She marched into the kitchen ten minutes early. Not only had the dough not risen but it looked like it had actually shrunk. "Damn! Damn! Damn! You little turd," she cried. "Why didn't you rise when I told you to rise? Do you think you're God almighty?"

Seizing the dough, she flung it against the wall over and over so violently that the bun on her head was undone and her hair tumbled freely over her shoulders. Even her stockings unrolled to her ankles. "I warned you," she cried as she grabbed the empty raisin container, shoved the dough into it, pounded the top on the container and hurled it into the waste basket. "Damn dough," she muttered as she wiped the perspiration from her brow, reached for a glass from the cabinet, poured herself some cooking sherry, and downed the whole glass without pausing once to get her breath. Passing the basket on her way to her bedroom, she stuck out her tongue at the raisin container with its sealed contents.

Once in her room she paused to look at herself in the mirror. Any other time she would have recoiled in horror at what she saw. Now, however, she stood admiring herself for several seconds. She marveled at how she had lost her composure, but she smiled freely at feeling so very good about what had happened. Then, without properly preparing herself, she plopped onto the bed and went off to sleep.

Priscilla awoke around three in the morning and decided she wanted a glass of milk. When she walked into the kitchen, she happened to glance at the wastebasket. "Noooo!" she gasped. The top of the raisin box had popped off from the pressure of the dough which had risen during the night and was now twice its size. It spilled out of its container and filled the basket. "But it couldn't...I mean, I didn't program it this way. It...it...but there it is! Well damn, damn, damn!" Priscilla laughed until the tears came down her cheeks. Holding high the container with its contents, she pirouetted several times around her kitchen. Then she removed the dough from the box and pushed it down on the counter for a second rising. She didn't know when the dough would rise again or even if it would at all. It didn't matter. She had learned something precious that night, and it had nothing to do with baking bread.

REFLECTION

Letting our light shine is not the same thing as flicking on a light switch. Turning on the light implies control, whereas letting the light shine suggests surrender and availability. "Letting" is not ordering or commanding the light to appear; rather, it is being there to receive it when it comes.

Undoubtedly, being in charge or in control is a value, and we mature by developing a strong ego whereby we can manage our lives more efficiently. But we can be so concerned with running our lives that the values of predictability, clarity, certainty, and orderliness become increasingly more important than what is novel, surprising, unpredictable, or mysterious. If there is no room for surprises in our lives, how then can we experience the Kingdom? Thus, Priscilla's need for propriety and orderliness is so inhibiting that in the rare moments when she experiences the freedom of the Kingdom in her own laughter and in slips of the tongue, she quickly moves the bushel basket back into place and promises to check any similar light moments from escaping.

However, even Priscilla can't keep the basket in place forever. The Kingdom arrives in its own time, not hers; and her response reveals her as a very human and lovable person.

Letting our light shine isn't a matter of calculation or control but one of surprise. We are there to receive the light, not to manufacture it.

Can we remember moments of surprise in our life when our light shone in unexpected ways? Might this help us be more receptive to future moments of being surprised by light?

PEARLIE

"Or again, the kingdom of heaven is like a merchant's search for fine pearls. When he found one really valuable pearl, he went back and put up for sale all he had and bought it." Matthew 13:45,46

"I'm not easy. I come at a price. I'm Pearlie, the girl of your dreams," she teased as she smiled coyly at Max.

"I know, I know," he conceded as they sat at a table in the elegant dining room of the *Gem Of My Life* restaurant. "I never said you were easy. And most certainly you come at a price, a great price," he laughed while he scanned the list of costly entrees. Setting aside the menu, he gently took Pearlie's hands and declared, "But Pearlie, you're the kind of girl I've always wanted to have—ever since I set eyes on you two months ago."

"To have?" Pearlie's eyes twinkled in the candlelight. Amused, she repeated, "Have?"

"Yes, have," he stated matter of factly.

Pearlie shook her head. He hadn't gotten the point of her question. Like the others she had dated, Max didn't seem to understand what he was asking of her. As she had with other men, however, she remained unruffled by his request. She knew what she had to do to enlighten him about winning her affection. Pearlie would play his game but she'd play it better than he did and maybe, just maybe, the two of them would both be winners. "So you want to have me, do you? And you understand the price is high?"

"Of course, of course. I understand," he answered waving his hand impatiently. "And I'm willing to pay the price—anything for you, Pearlie."

Little did Max know how much this pearl would cost. Even if he had known, it might not have made much difference. He had always been ready to pay for whatever he wanted in life. But he had failed to notice the costliness of his need to possess, and what this had done to him. He couldn't pass a bookstore without feeling compelled to buy a book. "I want to have that book; I must have it!" And once he had the book, he stored it with all the other unread books gathering dust on shelves throughout his house. He'd frequent fashionable clothing stores and within minutes need a fix. "I adore that suit. I want to have it. I'll pay anything for it." But, once in his possession, the suit was tucked away in one of several closets serving as graveyards for his clothes. He was always going on buying sprees. "That lamp! Those paintings! That mahogany dresser! I want to have them!" Store owners rushed to greet Max whenever he marched through their doors because they knew he'd be an easy mark.

Strangely, he was able to admire things before he possessed them. But once he owned something he never noticed it again. His acquisitions grew to occupy more and more space in his home. Paintings under beds and behind sofas. Two, three, and four lamps standing in corners like displaced persons waiting to be placed. Microwaves on top of microwaves crowding kitchen counter spaces. Statues of every conceivable size standing guard at every doorway in their house. There was so much clutter that he scarcely had room to move and breathe.

Since he met Pearlie, however, he was forced to change his ways. "I'm not easy. You want to have me? Then you pay the price. Let's dine tonight at the Ritz and drink the finest champagne available!" Which is what they did. "I want to shop at chic boutiques and buy designer clothes." Which is what they did. "Let's take a trip by jet—first class—to swim in Swaziland and see the wildlife in Kenya." And they did.

Max paid the price, all right. He wanted to have Pearlie badly. Oh, he wanted her so that he paid her bills piled high upon his desk. Sometimes he'd raise a finger and gingerly protest her spending sprees. Pearlie would simply smile, wink, and offer, "This is Pearlie you're talking to. I don't come cheap. Remember?"

How could he forget? But he had spent so much money by now that the only way he could pay her bills was by gradually selling off his possessions. Out went the books he had never read, the suits worn once at most, the furniture exiled to attic regions, and statues from every doorway.

However, a strange thing happened as he unmisered himself. Now that he knew he would no longer own things, he delighted in them as much as before he had impulsively purchased them. He fingered the books, opening and closing them, reading aloud from them before he placed them in boxes for the book dealers. Rediscovering long-abandoned suits, he admired them as he tried them on, and paraded up and down the room before finally sending them off to this or that pawn shop. He feasted his eyes on oriental rugs as he lifted layer after layer of patterned Chinese and Persian treasures off his floors. And sinking into overstuffed chairs or sitting for a last time on mahogany benches, he sighed over and over that he had never enjoyed these things so much as now when he would no longer have them as his own.

As he continued waving goodbye to his possessions, he wondered when he'd finally have his Pearl. When he put the question to her that way, she reminded him, "This pearl is not a piece of furniture. I'm not a collectible." And so she kept him in suspense. No, she wasn't easy, this precious pearl. Moreover, since he wanted to have her he would be forced to sell everything he owned. Because he now owned very little, it wasn't long before he had nothing left except for a few clothes and household items. To his amazement, though, having nothing didn't seem to bother him.

He could move about his house more freely and he thought he even breathed more easily now. "There's no more clutter here," he marveled. Moreover, no longer in need of buying something every minute of the day, he was free to see what he had never seen before: sunrises and sunsets, laughing children splashing water at one another in nearby lakes, multicolored patches of flowers in neighboring parks. With TVs, stereos, CDs, and VCRs gone, he found himself spending hours listening to the wind or rejoicing in the gently falling rain. He especially enjoyed the new time he found to stroll with old, long-neglected friends as well as new acquaintances.

Max had seen the writing on the wall for weeks. But now he found the courage to admit to Pearlie, "I can't keep it up. I don't have any more money. You're too costly. I've given up everything for you." And much to his surprise, he added, "Pearlie, I don't need to have you anymore. Even if I could pay, I'm not certain I would." Waves of relief came over him as the lifelong burden of needing to have was lifted from his shoulders. Looking into Pearlie's eyes, he confessed, "I guess it's over with us."

Pearlie took his hands in hers, gently kissed him on his lips, and whispered softly, "No, it's just beginning, Max. Pearlie is here to be with you. What do you say we go and waltz the night away?"

REFLECTION

Seeing things as they are and not as we would like them to be is a way of describing contemplation. We can "do lunch" with a view towards snagging a potential business partner, mate, enemy, etc. We're not approaching them as individuals in their own right. More often than not we see things in terms of our needs or their functions. We see an apple on a tree as being there for us to eat and not as something beautiful in itself. Looking at it as food is one thing. Regarding it apart from our need, however, we begin to consider its distinct shape, color, smell, and texture. We notice its proximate relationship to the branch on which it hangs as well as its more remote relationship to the other branches and the rest of the tree.

So being contemplative means being present to people and things in their own light and not in the light of our demands, whims, and expectations. If we are like Max it is difficult to be contemplative. "Possessions" have no value in themselves. Their worth depends on their usefulness to us. We notice them only when they break down or no longer work. When we treat children, spouses, lovers, and friends as possessions that we must jealously guard or as objects that are there to meet our needs, we no longer see them in their own light; we are not being contemplative.

Max was addicted to having. Fortunately, Pearlie helped Max detach himself from his need to have by leading him to believe he could have her for the right price, a price which was detachment itself. Once he became contemplative and no longer "needed" her, she paradoxically became available, not as a possession, but as Pearlie.

Being contemplative enables us to experience the luminosity of Being as it shines in each and every being's own distinct way. That is God's way of being there with us.

Is the pearl of great price something we discover in renouncing our need to have? And when does the desire for detachment itself become so intense that we become possessive in a new way? Is it possible to be so needy in our relationship with God that God becomes nothing more than a need-satisfier whose being is solely to be there for us?

THE TREASURE

"The reign of God is like a buried treasure which a man found in a field. He hid it again, and rejoicing at his find went and sold all he had and bought that field." Matthew 13:44

He was ecstatic! Had this happened to him? Maybe he was dreaming. But *no*. There was the gem box, corroded with rust, but still intact after having been buried for years in the rich soil. And the jewels in the box sparkled in the noonday sun: sapphires, rubies, diamonds, and other gems he couldn't even identify. Lester bit his lip so he wouldn't cry out for joy over his newfound discovery and arouse the suspicion of the others working in the field. Silently reviewing how he had come upon the treasure, he focused his attention on the opening in the ground. Lester had intended to drive long wooden stakes into the earth in order to establish boundaries marking off his rented portion of land from the others. What he could never have imagined was striking the metallic surface of the box with his shovel only minutes after he had begun digging.

"I'm a wealthy man! I'll never have to work again," he thought. "But I've got to calm down. The others must not see me walking off the property with this box." Lester knew that the gem box legally belonged to the landowner and there was only one way to claim the box as his own. "I'll buy the field. Yes, I'll buy the field and the box will be mine. It'll be costly. But these gems are worth fifty times what the land is worth." Addressing the box he whispered, "I'll have to bury you for a while, but I'll be back." Then he carefully replaced the box and covered it over with dirt. "And I'll draw a circle around you so I know where to find you," he confided as he traced a circle in the soil directly above the buried box. "There!" Rising to his feet, he gleefully rubbed his hands together and thought, "Wait until I tell Wanda and the kids about this!"

Lester bolted for home and on his way almost knocked over two friends. "Les, what's the hurry?"

"Sorry, can't talk now! I've got business to take care of."

His friends looked puzzled. "That's not like Les. He's always got time to stop and talk."

But there was no stopping Lester today. Once home he announced, "We're moving out of the house. We've got to sell it!"

"What?" Wanda exclaimed.

"No time for explanations. Get the pup tent out of the garage. That'll be our home."

"But, but..."

"Just for a while," he reassured her. "A couple of days. Then we'll buy a house ten times as big as this one. See you later," he added as he left his shocked wife and hurried to the realtor.

On the way Lester came across two more of his friends, drinking buddies from the local pub.

"Hi, Les. You going to join us today?" one of them asked. "I..."

"Sorry," Les interrupted. "I've got more serious things to do now. Maybe some other time. 'Bye, now!" And off he went.

"Les doesn't have time for a beer! That's surprising. He's always one for sitting around and having a good laugh," the friend commented.

"Yeah!" the other added. "Les is always telling us life is too short to be racing around without enjoying it." Then both of them looked on in silence as Lester disappeared down the street.

It took only two days for Lester to sell his house, get his life savings out of the bank, and purchase the land he wanted so desperately. "It's mine. The land is mine," he sighed as he kissed the deed to the land. "Now I'll get the gem box!" Lester hightailed it to the field even though a torrential rainstorm had begun the moment he had the deed in hand. Shrugging his shoulders, he muttered as he challenged the heavens, "No matter. No rainstorm can stop me." Or so he thought.

The heavy downpour, coupled with strong winds, had altered the landscape of the field. All of the stakes that had previously demarcated the plots were now strewn over the entire field. Arriving there, Lester was horrified. "The circle, the circle, where's the circle?" he panicked. Totally disoriented, he ran in every direction looking for the circle, which had long since been washed away. "Where is it? Where is it?" he moaned. Falling on his knees, he vowed, "I'll find you. A little digging will do it. You'll see!" A little digging?

Shovel in hand, Lester attacked the earth at a point where he hoped the treasure lay. But by evening he hadn't found the box. Exhausted, he leaned on his shovel and promised, "Tomorrow I'll be back with my family."

At the crack of dawn Lester, Wanda, and the kids straggled half asleep onto the field. They had brought with them their pup tent, food supplies, and shiny new tools. Lifting his shovel high, Lester gave the order. "Dig in! It won't take long to find the treasure but we can't fool around or laugh," he warned.

"But, Dad," one of the kids objected, "you're always telling us life is no fun if we don't have time to laugh."

"Yeah," Wanda chimed in. "He's right. Besides, do you see anyone laughing? Could anybody living in a pup tent laugh?" she cracked.

Lester waved away their questions. "OK, OK, let's get busy!" While Lester dug enthusiastically, the others poked around half-heartedly with their shovels.

Occasionally during the day a friend or acquaintance would drop by and try to strike up a conversation with Les or Wanda or the kids. Les would raise a hand and say, "No time for small talk. Gotta keep digging." By the end of the day they still hadn't found the box. "Well, we'll find it tomorrow," he told the tired family as they piled into their pup tent for the night.

And he told them the same thing each evening for the following two weeks as they dug and dug and dug without finding the treasure. More friends, neighbors, and relatives dropped by: sometimes to talk about the weather; sometimes to ask for advice; often to avoid being lonely. They had come to Les because in the past he had always been around to listen. But now he gave the same message to each and every person. "Can't talk! Gotta lot of digging to do!" Gradually, the number of visitors dwindled. Les had no time for what he considered idle chatter. "We've got to get that treasure. That's what counts. We don't have time for fooling around," he preached daily to his family as they dug and piled dirt upon dirt, making small hills over the entire field.

On the first morning of the third week Lester announced a new plan. "We're going to sift through all the dirt we've dug. We might have missed something."

"We might have missed something," the kids groaned.

Les hadn't expected the strong reaction. "Why, yes," he said softly.

"I'll tell you what we've missed," Wanda cried. Seizing her shovel, she hurled it as far as she could. Then she took off her shoes and socks, danced up and down the nearest hill, and then continued to do the same on the other hills.

"Yay! Yay! Yay! Go to it, Mom!" the kids chanted. Taking their cue from her, they too threw off their shoes and socks and ran in every direction onto different mounds of dirt. Slid-

ing, tumbling, jumping, and laughing, within seconds Wanda
and the kids had magically transformed the morbid field into
a joyous playground.

Lester was dumbfounded. He hadn't seen his children acting like children for such a long time that he didn't know
what to make of it. Nor had he ever seen Wanda so carefree.
His initial reaction was to order them all back to work. However, he momentarily forgot himself and chuckled as he
watched his wife pirouetting on a mound as the sun played
on her face. He had never seen her so lovely. Before he knew
it, he, too, had taken off his shoes and socks and was charging
up a hill. "Anyone want to play King of the Hill?" he laughed.
The last time he had been this happy was the day he had
found the gem box hidden in that field. "The treasure," he
thought. "I forgot about the treasure!" Then he giggled, wept,
and did a jig on top the hill. "Who cares about the buried
treasure?! Who needs it?!" Lester had found his treasure on
the field!

REFLECTION

Where is our treasure? What are we looking for? How
many miles are we willing to travel, how much time and money are we willing to spend to get what we want? And once we
get what we want, will we really be satisfied? More important, what will we have neglected and sacrificed in our single-
minded quest for our treasure?

Consider the following. A man decides to take a trip to a
beautiful park that he has never seen. His map tells him that
the park is fifty miles away. He must look for a sign that says:
The beginning of the park. He drives and drives, looking intently for the sign. There are beautiful trees, streams, and flowers
all along the way, but he is so preoccupied in his search for

the sign that he has no time for scenery. At long last he reaches a sign that reads: *This is the end of the park. We hope you have enjoyed your visit.* So intent was he on getting to the park that he didn't notice he had already been there!

We go through life looking for the treasures and we miss the treasures all along the way. We are always looking forward to some magical moment when we will find our treasure, e.g., graduation, marriage, the birth of a child, a raise in pay, etc. But our disregard or our blindness to the present moment prevents us from recognizing that the treasure is here in one another and in the events which make up our day-to-day living. The light is already shining in the present moment. What we need to do is open our eyes and hearts to its presence. To see the light shining now is already to have come out from under the basket.

Do we see it?

A FISH STORY

"The reign of God is also like a dragnet thrown into the lake, which collected all sorts of things. When it was full they hauled it ashore and sat down to put what was worthwhile into containers. What was useless they threw away." Matthew 13:47-48

They had been dragged into a room which appeared to be an antechamber to a larger room. Fins spread apart, two brightly-colored angelfish stood guard at the door to the inner room. Wearing reading glasses, a third angel sat at a desk with a stack of folders and a gavel. Raising the gavel, the angel pounded the table several times. "Order, order!" he cried. They were grumbling over how they had been caught in a net and dragged with all sorts of other creatures to this unknown destination.

"Now, now, don't take it personally, friends," the angel counseled. "Dragnets are currently the fastest way of gathering as many fish as possible."

"Boo! Boo!" His answer didn't satisfy the dogfish and catfish, the squid, sharks, sea squirts, bullheads, orange and blue roughys, snappers, snails, seahorses, and countless other fish in the room.

"What I want to know," snapped a sullen snapper, "is why we were hauled here in the first place?"

"I'd like an answer to that question, too," a roughy rumbled as he muscled his tattooed fins through the mess of fish to the front of the room.

Eyes bulging, a bullhead blustered, "Your reasons had better be good or else!"

"Here, here!" The angel pounded the gavel. "We've dragged you here because it's time to decide who's going to fish heaven. We're going to admit some of you and we're going to send the rest back."

"Fish heaven? Hey man, is that what's in the next room? Cool, real cool!" a catfish crooned.

"Yes, the angels at the door are prepared to open it for those who have lived good lives. And for those who haven't ...well, we have no alternative but to throw you back into the deep, dark waters."

"You mean where those mean looking, horny-headed devilfish hang out?" cried a frightened sea squirt.

"No, we think the devilfish only deserve one another. We wouldn't dream of sending you there. We'd just send you back to where we found you. There you could spend time getting your lives in order before we dragged you back here again," the angel explained.

"Ahhhh!" The fish were relieved. At least there was no need to worry about facing the devilfish!

However, everybody began to get excited at the prospect of going to fish heaven: some fish flipped their fins; the crabs moved forward, in reverse and sideways; the squid flailed their several arms, entangling themselves with anyone in reach; monkfish settled into chanting sea hymns and the sea urchins grew rowdier by the minute. Only the snail-slow snails and the clams remained calm at the possibility of going to heaven.

"How are you going to decide who's going to heaven? Who's going to make it and who isn't?" the fish fretted.

Pointing to the stack of folders, the angel answered, "Basically, by reviewing the data on how you've behaved toward

one another. For example, we note in our records that some of
the clams unfortunately preferred keeping silent when they
could have provided needed counseling for one of their deeply depressed sisters. On the other hand, other clams bravely
clammed up when their enemy tried to pry loose information
about a brother of theirs. They preferred a clambake rather
than betray a fellow clam." None of the clams commented on
the angel's observations. Given their taciturn nature, that was
understandable.

"I don't like what's happening here," blurted a bullhead.
"We didn't have time to prepare a defense."

"Even if you had spent months preparing a defense," the
angel countered, "it wouldn't have mattered in the least.
You've bullied your way through life by being offensive to
other fish who didn't see life as you swam it. In fact, this poor
shrimp next to you always suffered the indignity of your in-
sults. Isn't that right?"

The shrimp agreed as the bullhead shook an intimidating
fin at him. "Yes, the little shrimps of the world get it all the
time from these fellows. We're survivors, though, and we try
to support one another by looking out for one another."

"I know, I know," the angel smiled. "And because you
shrimp are so supportive of one another...well, you're going
to fish heaven today!"

"Really?" The shrimp was overjoyed.

"And what about me?" snarled a shark from a dark corner
of the room. Standing alone, the shark caused shivers to go up
and down the backbones of the other fish as he flashed razor-
sharp teeth at the angel.

"A lone shark!" the angel muttered. "You've taken advantage of others, threatened, maimed, and in some instances
killed them. You don't really think we consider you ready for
heaven, do you?"

"Just asking, that's all," the shark answered. "By the way,
you might want to have those angels at the door tail you
when you go outside. It's not safe out there, you know."

"Watch your mouth, buddy," warned a deep voice from the back of the room. The shark was ready to settle accounts but as he turned and faced his challenger, he retreated into his corner. A huge whale occupied the rear of the room.

"Thank you, sir," the angel applauded. "We know you're a whale of a fellow and even though you take up a lot of room, we've got plenty of space for you in heaven because you've always been willing to carry others on your back. True, now and then, you open up your mouth and swallow a few of your neighbors. But basically, you've done all right!"

The whale gushed a geyser of gratitude while the catfish ambled over to the angel and inquired, "Hey, man, am I in or am I not? I mean am I going to swim with the best of them or am I going to end up with sharkskin Sammy there?"

The angel imitated the catfish's tone and answered, "Well man, you've done such a good job cattin' around in your swimming hole that we figured you'd like cattin' around there for a few more years."

"Hey, that's fine with me, man. I got no hurry to leave my scene anyway. Just keep Sammy boy away from me," the cat purred, pointing to the lone shark who was nibbling on some poor fish bone.

"We'll see what we can do," the angel promised.

"What about us?"

"Who's that?" The angel strained to hear the voices. He scanned the room and then it dawned on him whose voices they were. Reaching for the microphone set aside for just such an occasion, he placed it in the middle of the room.

"What about us?" they repeated. This time the voices were clear and everybody recognized that the voices belonged to a school of minnows.

"You've had to suffer a lot," sympathized the angel. "Always being swallowed up or ending up on a nasty hook. The odds have never been in your favor. There's a place for you here where you don't need to be always on guard and where we think small is beautiful!"

"Whew!" The minnows were relieved and were presumably dancing somewhere in the room, although no one knew for sure since an anxious squid accidentally squirted an inky substance throughout the room, temporarily darkening it.

"Dare I ask where I stand?" a barracuda asked.

"You fellows gang up on others when they can't defend themselves. Need I say more?" the angel replied curtly.

"And what about me? I guess it's back to crabbin' on my home turf," one of the crabs crabbed. "After all, nobody cares about consorting with crabs. Why should it be any different in heaven?"

Quickly reviewing the crab's records, the angel said, "Yes, just the other day you were crabbing about overcrowding in your corner. I think..."

"No, he wasn't crabbing the other day," a carp interrupted. "You're mistaking him for me. I was carpin' about the crowds in my corner. He's not to blame," the carp insisted. "I wish you people would get the records straight!"

Carefully examining the name on the folder, the angel declared, "You're right!" and then he nodded in the crab's direction, "My apologies to you." Back to the carp, "And my admiration to you for confessing carping. For that bit of honesty you go to heaven...on condition that you and this crab take up residence next to one another to keep each other in check. You'll make perfect partners! If he crabs, you carp and if you carp, he crabs. OK?"

The crab and the carp sized up one another, shrugged their shoulders, and agreed to the conditions. Then the crab nudged the carp and whispered, "Maybe we can be a team, crabbin' and carpin'. We could even do a little soft shoe number since I'm a softshell crab. I'm sure the others would love to see our act."

"I'll think it over," the carp answered thoughtfully.

On and on throughout the night the fish raised their fins and inquired about their fate. Finally, after they had all been judged, the unlucky fish were ordered back into the net and dragged to their home waters. However, the fish who had been chosen to go to heaven remained in the antechamber until the two angels who had been guarding the door slowly pushed it open. Then the angels led all the saved fish into fish heaven.

"Ohhhh!" they marveled. They had been ushered into an unbelievably huge and beautiful fishbowl. There were dozens and dozens of fish bars with lovely gold bar stools throughout the fishbowl. In attendance were haloed goldfish bartenders in back of the bars waiting to serve the awestruck fish. The minnows, the shrimp, the whale of a fellow, the crab 'n' carp and all the other saved were simply overwhelmed by the splendor of their water paradise.

There was a trumpet blast, and a host of angelfish streamed past the saved towards a pearl-studded door (compliments of the heavenly pearl oysters). They opened it and, as the newly saved looked on in amazement, a simply stunning silver-bodied fish swam through the portal. Reflecting all the room's light on his body's silvery surface, the fish was dazzling, particularly where his body bore scars from earlier wounds. Majestically surveying all the saved, the silver fish, accompanied by the angels, swam over and said, "Brothers and sisters, from now on you can do what you do best—drink, drink to your heart's content. Drink like a fish, my friends! And let me be the first to serve you!" Two angels tied an apron around the silver fish's waist while the saved gathered on bar stools. Then the silver-bodied fish served them.

Soon the angels brought an apron to each of the saved so they could serve one another, too. Only the crab 'n' carp were excepted. They were preparing their soft shoe number for the evening's entertainment. The whole evening promised to be worth a lifetime's wait...and this was just the beginning of life in fish heaven.

REFLECTION

It's been said, "You are what you eat." We don't need to understand this literally to grasp the truth of the statement. We now know if we eat food high in cholesterol that our arteries get clogged. We know if people eat too many carrots, their skin turns orange. Just as there is truth in saying we are what we eat, there is also wisdom in stating that we are what we choose.

The choices we make during our lives move us in the direction of becoming certain kinds of persons. Psychologists tell us that as we age we become even more of what we had been earlier in life. Thus, if we chose to act kindly toward others early in the life cycle, chances are we will be kind later in life. Conversely, if we had acted cruelly toward others, then we become even more cruel as we age. What we end up doing through our choices is creating our own heaven and our own hell.

By heaven and hell we mean choices that either expand our concern for others or contract it to a narrow self-interest. By becoming what we choose, we either see ourselves as belonging to a larger reality (the world community, cosmos, God, etc.), or we identify ourselves as the sole reality that matters. Judgment can be understood within this context as self-imposed imprisonment, a self-absorption that is a living death.

The fish in this story are in some ways like people who choose to be who they are. Because of previous choices, some fish go one way and the rest go to the place of light. It must seem cruel that the bullheads, the lone shark, etc., don't get to fish heaven while the whale, the crab, and the carp, etc., do. Yet, it makes sense if we keep in mind that the label "bullhead" is not someone's external judgment as much as a statement of what this fish has chosen to be.

What cultural, familial, and personal predispositions have

entered into shaping our destiny? Can we still make choices that enable us to come from under the basket, or must these factors isolate us from everybody else? Our choice, like the fish in the story, is always whether to walk into the light or remain in the darkness.

THE CHOCOLATE MAN

Another time he said to his disciples: "A rich man had a manager who was reported to him for dissipating his property. He summoned him and said, 'What is this I hear about you? Give me an account of your service, for it is about to come to an end.' The manager said to himself, 'What shall I do next? My employer is sure to dismiss me. I cannot dig ditches. I am ashamed to go begging. I have it! Here is a way to make sure that people will take me into their homes when I am let go.'" Luke 16:1-4

"I can't go on this way! I've got to stop!" Lou declared. What did he have to stop? Eating chocolates, of course!

"This is too much! I've got to do something else for a living." What did he do for a living? Managed Bonnie's Best Bon Bons Chocolate Shop.

"Why am I doing this to myself?" What *was* he doing to himself? At 5 feet 5 inches, he weighed in at three hundred pounds! Yes, Lou had reason to be concerned about what had happened since he became the manager of the chocolate shop where they were made and sold. When Bonnie hired him a year earlier, Lou weighed only one hundred and fifty pounds.

At first the chocolates didn't tempt him. The trouble started slowly. One day he spied an oddly formed strawberry buttercream in a display case. "This should have been rejected," he thought as he snatched it out from among the others. Not wanting to waste it, he popped it into his mouth. "Ohhh! It's marvelous, simply marvelous, so smooth!" he moaned. And that did it. He was hooked!

In the days that followed he sampled all the chocolates— the creams, the pralines, the raisin and nut clusters. All of them! Hurrying to work each day, he could hardly wait to get his fix, secretly plucking freshly coated chocolates from trays and boxes. Filling his mouth he thought, "What else is there to live for?" Lou was very much a loner and had no close friends. The routine of going back to an empty apartment each night left him feeling empty. He could hardly wait to re-turn to work each day and be among his friends, the choco-lates.

He realized he needed to be more circumspect in satisfying his craving when he noticed employees eyeing him suspi-ciously when they discovered only seconds after they had filled the display case that all the coconut creams were miss-ing.

What Lou couldn't conceal was his burgeoning weight. Buying bigger and bigger shirts, trousers, belts, and under-wear, he thought, "This is terrible. I'm a living bon bon! I've got to stop!" But he didn't. Instead he consumed more and more chocolates on the job. And weekends were worse! Hoarding chocolates he had pilfered from the shop during the week, Lou prepared for his weekend binges. Chocolates, choc-olates everywhere! Under beds, in closets, bathtubs, coffee tins, and bread boxes. He'd sit in his rocker the whole week-end and gobble them up. By Sunday night the apartment was strewn with wrappers and empty boxes.

Then the inevitable happened. Returning to the shop after another lost weekend, he was summoned to Bonnie's office. "You're fired!" she told him. Sitting at her caramel-colored desk, she ticked off the times when workers saw him sneaking coconut creams. "We're not running this shop for you," she said. "As it is, we're barely breaking even. We don't even have enough money to advertise. Lou, you're killing yourself and the business! I'll let you stay two more weeks while you look for another job. In the meantime, keep your hands off the chocolates!"

Leaving her office, Lou was mortified. "What have I done? Eaten up their profits! And now I weigh a ton. People can't tell whether I'm rolling or walking when I come down the street. What am I going to do? Why, I can't even bend over to tie my shoelaces. How could I do any heavy work?" As Lou agonized over his prospects he noticed a customer as heavy as himself wave to the cashier. "Hmmmm," Lou wondered, "Does he have a chocolate problem, too?"

"I can't pay in cash! I don't have the funds right now," the customer was saying. "Can't you charge the chocolates once more for me? Please?"

"He has a problem, all right," Lou thought. "He's probably deep in debt from eating so much. I feel sorry for him. I wish there were something I could..." Lou paused, his eyes lit up, "I know! I've got it! I've got it!" Lou waddled over to the customer and tapped him on the shoulder. "Hey, buddy, how would you like it if we cut your bill in half?"

"Huh? What?" The man was taken off guard. "Sure, I'd love it! But what's the catch?"

"Well the owner needs to advertise this place...and I notice you are a little on the stocky side like me."

"So?" the customer puzzled.

"So...suppose the two of us get sandwich boards and advertise Bonnie's Best Bon Bons in the city square. You can work off half, maybe even more of what you owe just by strolling through the square. People could hardly miss seeing us and they'll sure get the point that the chocolates must be pretty good!"

"Well..."

"And besides, we can get acquainted and get a little exercise at the same time. It's worth a try, isn't it? So what do you say?"

"OK, OK. I'll try it. But if I feel foolish, forget it!"

"Of course, of course. And if I find a few others like us, I'll see if I can get them to join us."

During the next couple of days Lou managed to strike the same deal with a few more overweight customers who couldn't pay their bills. At noon the next Monday, six of them marched into the city square. Initially, they felt silly since they practically filled the square with their bodies, and their huge waistlines made the sandwich boards practically stick out in front and back. Lou occasionally had to encourage the others, because some of the bystanders made nasty remarks about their weight. "Hey, fatso—are you bon bons full of nuts or raisins or what?" However, most of the people chuckled and quite a few curious onlookers visited the chocolate shop.

More important, the men began sharing their concerns with one another as they walked. They talked about how they had hoped to forget their problems by eating chocolates and how depressed they were because they felt so worthless. By the third day, they had bonded and now referred to themselves as "The Bon Bon Boys." By week's end their discussions had been so helpful that they decided to lengthen their advertising sessions by an hour!

On Friday, Bonnie called Lou into her office. "Lou, I'm amazed at what you've accomplished. At first I thought your advertising stunt was crazy and I was going to fire you immediately. Not only for parading around in the square but for reducing the bills of our biggest customers without even asking!! But within the hour the number of customers had increased twenty-five per cent and now we are selling more chocolates than ever. You're shrewd, Lou, very shrewd. I would like you to stay here. We need you!"

Lou smiled from ear to ear. Yes, he was shrewd, but he wasn't certain he could continue working next to all the coconut creams in the shop. Yet he now had friends who supported him and he felt he had the courage to deal with his problem. "Let me think about your offer," he said. "Maybe I'll come back, but only if I can wear very heavy mittens!" he laughed. "In any case, I've got to talk it over with the Bon Bon Boys!"

REFLECTION

The only way to make a figure eight is by going down, under, over, and up. There's no way but down and, once down, it's back up again. Once completed, the figure eight makes sense. Down, under, over, and up also describes the process of conversion. We move from being on top to hitting rock bottom before we can move back up again to complete the process of transformation. Stated another way, we initially experience relative stability in our lives, then instability, confusion, and a period of being down, at our wit's end, in the pits, etc. Only then do we begin to come back up into the light of day and restabilize with a new perspective on life. Paradoxically, we come out from under the basket by first going down under, being there for a while, and then coming up from under.

However miserable Lou is, as long as he manages to get along minimally at home and at work he isn't likely to change for the better. He changes only when he is grossly overweight and is fired from his job. Only then is he able to comprehend what he has done to himself, the predicament he is in, and the necessity of changing the direction of his life. Fortunately, he is able to find support "down under" from others who share his problem.

Bonding is a special kind of support. In conversion experiences those who support us best are generally themselves in need of similar support. *Alcoholics Anonymous, Parents Anonymous,* and *Narcotics Anonymous* are examples of groups that recognize the power of bonding when people are in desperate straits. Bonding is done at the "bottom," because only when we are stripped of our illusions and brought low can we share what is left to share: the empathy of our common humanity. When bonding takes place we are already on our way up from under. Why? In the bonding we discover a sense of worth, self-esteem, and the possibility of a new vision for life. However brightly our light may have shone before the conversion, the best is yet to be!

Lou faces problems in his future. He's still got a long way to go. But now he has the strength and the support of others. Against this background, his light is able to shine. And because he helped others' lights to shine, his shone all the brighter.

When have we looked to others for help? When have we been helped so that we experienced light in our lives? Could this have happened if we hadn't reached out to others? Is this the step we need to let our light shine?

GIVEAWAY

Jesus said to his disciples: "A rich man had a manager who was reported to him for dissipating his property. He summoned him and said, 'What is this I hear about you? Give me an account of your service, for it is about to come to an end.' The manager thought to himself, 'What shall I do next? My employer is sure to dismiss me. I cannot dig ditches. I am ashamed to go begging. I have it! Here is a way to make sure that people will take me into their homes when I am let go.'" Luke 16:1-4

"It's for you. It matches your eyes."

"Take it! It's yours. It goes with your hair."

"This will cheer you up. It fits you perfectly." What was Ted Ballows giving away? Sapsucker shirts from the Sapsucker showroom on the fourth floor of the Sapsucker Brothers Building in Chicago. Ted had been hired by the brothers ten years ago, at age fifty, to promote Sapsucker shirts to prospective buyers by escorting them through the showroom where the new lines of shirts were displayed.

Ted loved his job. "I like working there because I love to meet people," he told friends. And the Sapsucker brothers were happy to have Ted as an employee because his warm, inviting smile and hearty laugh helped employees and visitors alike to feel at home. "Ted is easy to talk to," Sam Sapsucker told his brother. "Right, Sam!" Steve agreed. "He's a real asset to the company."

What the brothers didn't know was that Ted was making Sapsuckers a home for more people than prospective buyers. He freely gave away shirts, sweaters, and bathrobes to friends, friends' friends, relatives, and relatives' relatives. Not that any of these people had come for a handout. Oh, no. They came to Ted because they were attracted by his warm, inviting smile and hearty laugh or they had heard he listened to everyone with a sympathetic ear.

People just stopped in at the showroom. "Hi, Ted, you don't know me. I'm Bill Quick, a friend of your friend, Mary Nelson. She told me to come and see you. Uhhh...could I talk to you?" That's generally the way a story began. Or "Hi, Ted, I'm Joe Smith, your brother-in-law's cousin. If you have a little time, could I tell you what's bothering me? You see, I've got this problem..." And then the visitor poured out his heart and soul as Ted listened attentively. Once a visitor had told his story Ted gave an encouraging word, a hug, and surprised the person with, "How would you like a smart Sapsucker shirt? It'll make you look snappy!"

"Why...why, why, yes, that would be nice," the startled visitor answered. The people who came to Ted were always relieved when they left because they had found someone who listened to them. However, it didn't hurt to walk out of the building carrying the best brand in the land. A Sapsucker!

Even people who had no intention of visiting Ted were treated to a Sapsucker. Assuming many of the visitors in the building were friends' friends or relatives' relatives, Ted stopped complete strangers in hallways, elevators, waiting rooms, washrooms, or wherever, and introduced himself. He disarmed them so completely with his pleasing personality that before they knew it they, too, were talking to him about their lives. He'd invite them to the showroom for a cup of coffee, a slice of banana yogurt bread, and would cap the meeting with, "How would you like a Sapsucker?"

Ted had given away so many Sapsuckers over the years that no one was certain when they saw someone wearing the Sapsucker label whether the person had bought the shirt or gotten it as a gift from Ted.

After Ted had been with Sapsuckers for ten years a change occurred in his life. When he had begun working with the company, he had gone through a difficult divorce. Badly hurt by the ordeal, Ted had periodic bouts of depression that he concealed pretty successfully. Now, however, the bouts were more frequent. More and more, he neglected his appearance. Hair disheveled, trousers wrinkled, and Sapsucker shirts no longer spotlessly clean, Ted holed up in his Seventh Avenue apartment for hours on end. He wanted to spend more and more time in bed. Getting up and going to work became a real chore. Life became a bore, a bummer.

All this came to a head the day Ted announced to his friends, "Well, I'm going to be fired! Wait and see. I've given away too many Sapsuckers!"

"Did the Sapsucker brothers say you were going to be fired?" they asked.

"No, but it will happen! In a couple of days," he nodded gravely. However, a couple of days passed and nothing happened. "Tomorrow, tomorrow it will happen," he solemnly assured his friends. "Yup, tomorrow is the day." But that day came and went and nothing happened.

"Why weren't you fired?" a friend asked.

"They don't fire employees on St. Vitus Day," he answered. "But tomorrow...just wait and see." But another day passed and still nothing happened.

"Why didn't the Sapsuckers fire you this time?" they asked.

"One of the Sapsucker brothers is out of town. That's why! But tomorrow when he gets back, *then* it will happen."

"Oh?" His friends were growing suspicious. And they were particularly disturbed when Ted told them the Sapsucker brothers were holding off firing him until the FBI concluded its own investigation. Looking over his shoulder he'd whisper, "They want to know how many Sapsuckers I've taken before they put the finger on me. I'm convinced they're spying. Their van is across the street from my apartment. I've seen them using binoculars to trail me."

By now his friends were very worried and they tried to persuade Ted that he needed to get rest and go into a hospital for treatment. But Ted could not be persuaded. He was convinced that the day of reckoning was right around the corner. Over and over he imagined the Sapsucker brothers confronting him. He created different scenarios as to what might happen when they spoke.

"You're fired! We'll see to it that you spend the next twenty-five years at hard labor to make up for the Sapsuckers you've given away!" or "We'll force you to learn Korean and sew each Sapsucker by hand in our factories over there...until you're 107!" or "We demand you go to all the people you've given Sapsuckers to and ask them back."

"Oh," Ted groaned, "that would be the worst punishment of all!" He'd have to go to half the people in Chicago for that! After rehearsing all the ways he could be punished, Ted exclaimed, "What's wrong with me? Am I crazy?" His friends tried to convince him that if he didn't go to a hospital soon, not only would he be crazy; he'd drive them crazy, too! Finally, he agreed to enter the hospital.

Ted hadn't been there more than two days, however, when he was getting visitors from all over the city. Men and women who had met Ted at Sapsuckers lined up to see him, decked out in their Sapsucker shirts and sweaters.

"Why all the Sapsuckers?" Dr. Smucker asked a nurse.

"They're all coming to see Ted Ballows, Doctor. They're his business associates, his friends, his friends' friends, his relatives, and his relatives' relatives. It's remarkable!" But what was even more remarkable was Ted's recuperation. No one had ever recovered as quickly in the whole history of the hospital. Why? "I found out how many people love me," Ted explained to a friend. And he no longer worried whether the Sapsucker brothers would fire him. "There will always be people who will take me into their homes. I know that now," he said. But....surprise! The Sapsucker brothers sent Ted a bouquet of flowers that practically filled his room. "We miss you. Come back soon," the card read. Ted's eyes filled with tears. "The Sapsuckers want me back...I'm going back to the Sapsuckers!" Beaming, he left his room. Passing a particularly troubled person on the stairs, Ted asked, "Do you want to talk? I'm a good listener, and...by the way, how would you like a Sapsucker shirt? I happen to have an extra with me!"

REFLECTION

It's striking how Jesus' parables are so free of religious language. There is no talk of God, grace, or faith in the great stories of the *Prodigal Son*, the *Good Samaritan*, the *Workers in the Vineyard*, etc. And Jesus never describes characters who are good to one another "because they see God in someone" or because they are motivated by good intentions. No, he concentrates on how people deal with one another regardless of intention. What finally saves someone from destruction is how that person acts toward another human being.

Talk about purity of motive isn't an issue; results are. The unjust judge will act justly because he needs his rest and he won't get it from the nagging widow. The owner of the vineyard is good to all his workers and it is his goodness that counts, not his motives. Maybe Jesus recognizes that we can be too much concerned with motivation and too little concerned with results. His admiration for results is nowhere more apparent than in the parable of the dishonest manager. The manager knew how to "save" himself by being good to the people who could help him. We question the manager's motives and Jesus praises what he does!

Of course Ted Ballows can be faulted for his cavalier giveaway program, but...he was doing good. Perhaps even the Sapsucker brothers benefited from the advertising! Moralists might argue about achieving a moral end through immoral means. But when lives are touched in the way Ted touched those who came to see him...well, what can we say? The fact is Ted Ballows's light shone all over Chicago. That ought to count for something!

Do we prevent our light from shining because others might call into question our motives for doing what we do? Isn't *doing* good far more important than *why* we do good?

JOANNA

On one occasion when a great crowd was with Jesus, he turned to them and said, "If anyone comes to me without turning his back on his father and mother, his wife and his children, his brothers and sisters, indeed his very self, he cannot be my follower." Luke 14:25

"Joanna and Chuza? They're made for one another!"

"Joanna and Chuza? The perfect couple!"

"Joanna and Chuza? A match made in heaven!" Yes, when anyone in Herod's court spoke of Herod's finance minister, Chuza, Joanna's name was invariably mentioned. "They belong together—like two peas in a pod," a court official chortled.

"Inseparable—like Siamese twins," another added. Joanna and Chuza had been married twenty years. He had been minister to Herod for five and Herod was delighted every time Joanna accompanied her husband to the court social functions.

"How charming," Herod observed on several occasions as Chuza beamed and Joanna blushed.

"See what the king thinks, Joanna, my Joanna," Chuza would say. "I'm proud of you! My Joanna, my little kitten!"

"I'm pleased as punch to make you proud," she'd purr.

"We envy you," other officials said when Chuza brought his elegant and lovely Joanna to their homes. "How witty! What class!"

"Ah, yes, she's my Joanna," Chuza smiled proudly. Then he'd whisper excitedly, "Joanna, see...see what they think of you! You're my girl, my Joanna, my pigeon!"

"Anything to please you, love," Joanna cooed.

People never tired of dishing out compliments and as the years rolled by Chuza made certain that he always brought his Joanna with him. And Joanna? Did she ever tire of the endless round of social events and compliments? Not in the beginning. However, recently she had begun to feel bored and restless. And on one occasion after Chuza praised his Joanna for pleasing him, she snapped, "I'm not your Joanna!" Startled, Chuza asked, "Wha...what is wrong Joanna?"

"Nothing...nothing...I don't know," she said, her eyes moistening. Chuza shrugged his shoulders and dismissed the outburst. However, the following evening at Herod's court, he would do more than shrug in reaction to what Joanna did there.

Herod threw a dinner party and during the party, Salome, the daughter of Herodias, Herod's wife, danced in the king's presence. She so delighted him that he promised her whatever she desired. Salome left the room for five minutes and then returned requesting the head of John the Baptist. Surprised by her request, Herod hesitated, but finally ordered the prophet's head be delivered to the banquet hall instantly. Joanna's face turned ashen white. She had never met the Baptist but she admired him for publicly speaking against Herod's illicit marriage to Herodias. She hadn't spoken of her admiration to her husband, because she hadn't wanted to displease him. However, Herod's order to kill the Baptist repelled her. "I want to leave," Joanna told her husband. "Now!"

"Joanna, Joanna, we can't leave. What would the others say if we left the party before the king had gone?"

"I don't care what they'd think! I can't stomach this!"

Tightly holding her hand, Chuza said coldly, "My Joanna, I need you at my side. My elegant, my charming Joanna, how will I look without you?"

"How will you look?" Joanna's eyes widened. "Do you see that mirror?" she asked, pointing to a wall of mirrors in the entrance. "Find out for yourself!" she cried, wrenching her hand from his. Then she darted out of the room as several persons, including Herod, watched.

Herod approached the embarrassed Chuza. "Where did your Joanna go?"

"Uh, she has a fever, your majesty. She had to leave."

"Oh?" Herod didn't seem convinced. "Don't you think you should be with her?"

"Yes, of course," Chuza said. He hesitated, then added, "My apologies, your majesty. With your permission, I take my leave," and he made a hasty retreat from the hall.

Shortly he caught up with Joanna and demanded, "Why have you done this? Don't you realize what this can do to my career? My future?"

Joanna halted, looked intently into Chuza's eyes and answered, "I see more clearly than I ever have what being your Joanna has done to me and how it will destroy me if I keep living this way. What do you think I am? Some kind of pet or good luck charm?" Joanna winced and shook her head. "For years it gave me pleasure to please you!"

"And now? Pleasing me doesn't matter?"

"No! Not when it displeases me to see Herod destroy a man on a girl's whim! Especially a man who spoke his conscience! And all you care about is what you'll look like without me at your side. That's when I stop being your Joanna!"

Chuza's face reddened. "Oh? Is that so? Who do you think you'll be without me? Take a little time to think about what you've just said and maybe you'll reconsider!" Turning on his heel, Chuza marched off into the night.

For the next couple of days Joanna pondered what had happened. She had surprised herself. What she suspected but never clearly understood until the night she had contradicted her husband was that she was no more than an ornament in his life. But now she knew she had to lead her own life. Yet she wondered if she was being too headstrong. "What am I doing? Being selfish? Am I out for myself? Only myself?"

Struggling with these questions, she happened upon a small crowd gathered on a street corner listening to a young man. Curious, she walked over to a woman in the group, tapped her on the shoulder, and asked who was speaking. "He's Jesus of Nazareth," she answered.

"Jesus? Another outspoken prophet," Joanna thought. "I've heard of him. He speaks his mind like the Baptist."

"Friends," the man said, "if any of you wants to join me, I invite you to do so. But you'll have to say no to those who want to stop you. That could mean your parents, your brothers and sisters, yes, even your spouse. There's pain involved in deciding, but if you're not willing to embrace pain for the sake of the kingdom, then it's better if you stay home."

His voice was gentle but firm and his words weren't lost on Joanna. "He's read my mind," she gasped. "He knows my anguish! I must hear more!" And Joanna listened to him. She began to follow him wherever he preached. It wasn't long before she met two other women, one named Mary Magdalene and the other, Suzanna. The three followed Jesus. She was no longer Chuza's Joanna. No longer did she strive to please him. Now it pleased her to follow Jesus. She was now her own Joanna.

REFLECTION

Whose life are we living? Whose light is shining? We can live for years doing what others expect without ever really knowing what is in our own deepest interest. We can live not only with others but for them. As a result, we achieve no self-identity, no sense of separateness. One reason we live so attached to others is our fear of not surviving on our own. "You can't make it," or "You're helpless without me," or "Let me take care of you" are the messages we hear when we try to differentiate from our families of origin, our friends, spouses, or organizations. Unfortunately, these messages never help us mature.

Maturing means achieving both communion with and separateness from others throughout the life cycle. The failure to achieve communion is a failure in intimacy while the failure to achieve separateness is a failure in identity. It isn't unusual for those of us in midlife to realize we haven't been living our own lives. Overly dependent on spouses or others as sources of self-worth, we do whatever is in our power to please them. We must continually win approval of ourselves and of what we do or we become paralyzed. Overly concerned with what elderly parents may think of us, we dare not risk offending them. In either case, our excessive need to please means never really choosing what accords with our own real needs and aspirations. In other words, we live others' lives while our own light is hidden under another's basket.

Joanna illustrates a middle-aged person who takes the first, painful step out from under the basket of another's identity in order to find herself. It is painful because she feels guilty and anxious as she takes the step. Like Joanna, we sometimes have to embrace uncomfortable feelings of guilt, anxiety, and loneliness as we become the persons we are called to be. In addition, we have to embrace this "cross" if we are to experience our light as our own and not as a satellite to someone else's.

In growing up, have we ever felt it vital to distinguish who we were from parents, friends, lovers, etc.? In spite of the pain, did we recognize the necessity of taking these steps if we were to experience our own light? Do we see the possibility of making similar choices in the future?

GOING PLACES

"For everyone who exalts himself shall be humbled and he who humbles himself shall be exalted." Luke 14:11

"Do you want to climb the ladder of success?"
"Oh, yes!"
"Do you want to be at the top?"
"Certainly!"
"Do you want to move in high places?"
"Without a doubt!"
"Then look sharp. Watch your step. Play the game. Follow the rules. Then you'll get ahead."

As far back as he could remember Abe had gotten advice for advancing himself socially and professionally. Since he had been so intent on moving up, he paid attention to what friends, relatives, and associates told him. "Abe, when you are with your elders, smile a lot, and listen carefully. Don't interrupt when they are speaking and don't be disagreeable with them. You don't want them upset," Abe's father admonished him.

Abe smiled, listened carefully, didn't interrupt or disagree with him.

"You see? You see?" his dad chortled. "You are going places, believe me!"

"You want the girls should like you, Abe?" his mother asked, rocking in her rocker.

"Yeah, Ma," Abe answered eagerly.

"Then be strong, smile a lot, tell them you're crazy about the bagels they bake, but don't talk with food in your mouth! Understand?"

"Yeah, I..."

"And wear clean pants and underwear! Cover up the zits on your face, chew peppermint before kissing a girl, and oh, yes, don't talk with your mouth full! Understand?"

"Sure, Ma," Abe said as he looked in the mirror for telltale pimples, checked his pants and underwear, put peppermints on his must-have list, returned to the mirror, and practiced smiling boldly saying, "I love your bagels! I bet your little hands have been busy baking bagels for hours! I love your bagels! I bet your little hands..."

"You see? You see?" his mother beamed. "You're going places! You're going places! Wait and see!"

"You want that God should help you? That his face shine on you?"

"Oh, by all means, rabbi!" Abe said.

"Well then, say your prayers, go to synagogue, hang around with the right kind of people, don't get smart with the elders, eat clean, be clean, check your underwear and, above all, watch your mouth with you know who if you know what is good for you," the rabbi concluded, pointing heavenwards. "Understand?"

"Sure, sure," Abe said as he checked his underwear, muttered prayers, reviewing whether he knew enough or needed to know more.

"Should you do all I have told you, you will most certainly go places," the rabbi nodded gravely.

Abe got even more advice from comedy writers, natural food nuts, haberdashery clerks, and poise perfectionists: from comedy writers on jokes that sailed and jokes that flopped; from the food nuts on the brans he ought to eat to give nature a little help; from clothiers on the cut and color of suits calculated to advance his career; and from poise perfectionists on how to pose and be composed as he positioned himself to move to the top.

"Sure, sure," he said over and over. And over and over, the words echoed, "You've got a future. You're going places!"

Primed with so much advice and decked out in designer clothes, he ought to have successfully launched his career the day he was invited to attend a banquet at which Jesus of Nazareth was to be present. Big shot politicians and religious leaders were to be in attendance. So, too, the directors from the local community theaters! They were always looking for new talent and Abe was excited about them being present. After all, he had been acting for so many years he felt he had a good shot at getting a part in a play.

When he arrived at the home where the party was being given, he began to panic. Was he ready for all of this? Perspiring, he momentarily excused himself, went to the rest room, checked out his smile in front of the mirror, rehearsed a few prayers he had learned to impress the religious folk, checked his underwear, popped a peppermint in his mouth, rechecked his underwear and, assuming an air of nonchalance, he reentered the room.

Smiling at anyone who looked in his direction, he seated himself next to an elderly gentleman. Still smiling, he cocked an ear toward the old gentleman who appeared to be whispering something to him. "What was that?" Abe asked. "Could you please speak a little louder?" The old man leaned closer to Abe but he still couldn't understand him. Straining both to keep smiling and understand the old man, Abe said, "I still can't hear you; please speak louder."

"I said," the old man yelled as everybody turned and listened, "You are sitting in the guest of honor's place. You'll have to go somewhere else! Need I say more?"

Abe was stunned. His smile froze as his face turned crimson. "I...I...I...," he stammered, rising to his feet and accidentally tripping on the back of the old man's robe. Quickly retreating to an open place far, far away from where he had been sitting, Abe fell into a little heap, eyes downcast, wishing with all his heart he were invisible. Mortified, he contemplated his future. Once the word had gotten around about what had happened he couldn't possibly get to the top. He was going nowhere!

No sooner had this thought taken possession of him than someone cheerily advised, "If you really want to get to the top, why don't you sit in the kind of place you are now, with the nobodies, about as far from the head table as possible? You'd be surprised what can happen. You might get invited to sit next to the somebodies. Then everybody will say, 'Somebody likes him; look where he's being seated! He must be somebody. He's really going places!'"

Abe turned his head toward a young man sitting next to him. He was nibbling a Ritz cracker. Grinning, the man continued, "Anyway, the important thing to remember is if you're always trying to make it big and go to the top, you've got to play too many games. Then you're bound to feel tied up in knots, and that leads nowhere but down, down! But if you stop playing games, you can really have fun just playing at being you and not someone you're not. Sounds great, doesn't it? A line I like that sums it up nicely is 'Those who exalt themselves shall be humbled and those who humble themselves shall be exalted!' Sounds more Chinese than Jewish, but it's true nonetheless."

The man laughed and it was so infectious that Abe laughed too! He hadn't laughed this freely in years. In fact, he hadn't ever been on this kind of a high. He realized he probably was never going to the top after today, but now that didn't seem to matter so much.

"Jesus! Jesus!" The old man who had told Abe to move was waving his hand. "Come up here! This seat is for you!"

"No, I'm just fine where I am! I'm having a great time with my friend," the man next to Abe said as he placed his arm around Abe's shoulder. Abe's mouth dropped open. This man talking to him was Jesus of Nazareth.

"Well, I'll be!" Abe cried, tears coming down his cheeks. "This fellow Jesus obviously enjoys himself wherever he's at and he has no need to get to the top!" Abe thought. He laughed. "I guess he's already there!" Then Abe sat back, relaxed, and enjoyed the view from the top with Jesus.

REFLECTION

Great performers are called stars. As we know, stars shine. But the star's light is derived from a good performance, and not necessarily from the performer's personality. We can marvel at a brilliant performance by Vanessa Redgrave in *Orpheus Descending*, but her performance doesn't give us a clue regarding her personal incandescence. Likewise, a hack performer may radiate a personal light of which only a few close friends are aware. While the difference between a brilliant stage performance and personal brilliance may be of minor interest to most of us, the difference between the performances we deliver in our daily lives and our true stellar qualities ought to be of primary interest to all of us. Why?

Because mistaking our performances for our selves hides our light under the basket of pretense even if the performance is a good one. And many of us are performing without knowing it. Like Abe, we have been prompted from an early age on how to talk, listen, feel, and react in a variety of situations. We have been coached into acting in certain ways in public to win what we or someone else wants for us. Our scripts come from parents, friends, relatives, schools, synagogues, churches, government, etc. Often, without realizing it, we are reading the lines and going through the motions dictated by the script.

At some point in the life cycle it is important to consider whether the words we speak, the choices we make, and the actions we perform are our own or those of someone in performance. For however brilliant the performance, if we get lost in someone else's script, then our light will remain hidden under the basket as we live lives of inauthenticity.

The question comes down to this: Who's the shining star? The person or the performer?

NEW WORLD

Martha, who was busy with all the details of hospitality, came to him and said, "Lord, are you not concerned that my sister has left me to do the household tasks all alone? Tell her to help me."

Luke 10:40

"Mary, stop eavesdropping. What they're talking about is no concern of yours. I need you here to mash the potatoes."

"Mary, have you got your ear against the keyhole again? What for? What they're talking about is Greek to us. Help me make the soufflé."

"Mary, you've got your foot in the door again. I know what you're up to. Menfolk's business is men's, not ours. Let's do the dishes and chat about the weather."

Martha shook her head. Over and over she reminded her sister that what was on the other side of the kitchen door wasn't any of their business but their brother Lazarus's and the men whom he had invited to their house to discuss the heavy stuff: politics, affairs of state, religion. "We've got other things to do, you and me. Putting the Swedish meatballs side by side with cheese 'n' crackers, sending our turkey and cranberries out on time, and being available when we're called upon to serve second helpings or whatever else tickles their fancy."

Mary needed no reminders. But she wondered, "What's wrong with me? Why can't I be happy here in the kitchen where I belong? Why don't I delight in dicing carrots or whipping up mile-high meringues? Why can't I find the joy in cooking and celebrate cuisine? Everybody—Martha, Lazarus, the girls, my rabbi—they all tell me the folly of wanting more and wanting to be more than I'm entitled to. But I do want more, so much more than compliments for doing what others say we do best—kitchen work."

That's why Mary couldn't be pressured by her sister to stay away from the door that separated them from the unknown world that only the men inhabited. Although she couldn't make out what they were saying, every now and then she overheard a word or two about who was running for an office, what interpretation a rabbi gave to a point about the law, etc. The little she heard made her all the more eager to hear.

Whenever she had an excuse to enter the room where Lazarus and his friends carried on, she'd do so. "Does anyone want anything to drink?" or "Maybe I could get you more cheese 'n' crackers?" or "If it's too hot in here, I can open the windows." Periodically Lazarus glared at Mary and she realized she had gone too far. Retreating to the kitchen, she found no comfort from Martha.

"You don't belong there! You don't belong," Martha wagged. Humiliated by what her curiosity had prompted her to do, Mary then worked doubly hard in the kitchen: mixing even higher mountains of meringue; peeling potatoes by the bushel. But the more she applied herself to kitchen tasks, the greater her passion was to discover the world in the other room.

Then it happened. One day Lazarus announced, "Jesus is coming. He's the popular rabbi causing all the stir these days. A few of my friends will be joining us for dinner. Prepare something special."

Mary had heard of Jesus and she was overjoyed he was coming to their home. She wanted to see and hear him, but she knew she'd see and hear little unless...unless. Mary's eyes lit up. "Yes, yes, I know what I will do," she thought.

On the day Jesus came to dinner, Mary and Martha had outdone themselves in preparing a magnificent dinner. Before the dinner, they had poured wine into a decanter and Mary quickly offered to serve the guests. No sooner had she entered the room, however, than she appeared to spill some of the wine on the floor accidentally. "Oh, I'm so sorry," she apologized profusely. "Just go on talking. I'll clean it up. It will only take a minute." She just happened to have a wet cloth with her, and she got down on her hands and knees and began slowly wiping up the wine. At first no one noticed her. Jesus was talking about how the barriers between the rich and the poor had to be destroyed and that there was room for everybody around God's table.

"And I'll tell you another barrier that has to go," Mary blurted as she finished wiping the wine off the floor. Horrified, she brought her hand to her mouth. Had she said that? Slowly raising her head, she saw Lazarus's face reddening and the other men harrumphing and sputtering—except Jesus. He was smiling.

"What other barrier did you have in mind?" he asked.

Mary slowly rose to her feet. "I...I..." At a loss as to what to say or do, she began to retreat towards the safety of the kitchen. But Jesus raised his hand.

"No, wait! Please come and join us. Sit with us. I would like to hear what you have to say." The other men were dumbfounded but didn't dare to protest Jesus' invitation. Warily, Mary walked a couple of feet toward where Jesus sat. Sitting at his feet, she quietly pointed to the kitchen and said, "Why rabbi, I mean the barrier between that room and this one."

"Ah, yes," Jesus agreed. "You are right. It has existed way too long."

No sooner had he said this than Martha barreled through the door. Her face flushed with anger, she exploded, "Rabbi, would you remind that sister of mine that there's work to be done in the kitchen?"

"Calm down, Martha," Jesus said. "Mary has made her choice. She wants to be here. Let's not deny her what's better for her. If you want to come and sit down, join us. We'll all be glad to come and help you later. Right, fellas?" The men looked at one another in disbelief. They had no idea what helping out in the kitchen would mean since they had hardly ever entered one before. But at least for that evening they, too, were going to take a journey to another world. Without so much as glancing up at Jesus, they responded to Jesus' question by mumbling, "Right!"

But Martha could not be persuaded to remain and she marched back into the kitchen muttering, "This is where I belong."

"Now where were we, Mary?" Jesus asked. "Oh yes, those barriers. They have to go. Have you anything else you'd like to say?"

Mary beamed. She was home.

REFLECTION

Many women react negatively to Mary. After all, *someone* has to prepare the meal! They resent Jesus' apparent dismissal of Martha's complaint that Mary isn't doing her share of the kitchen duties. However, our story enables us to understand Mary's action as courageous and not as self-serving. Her light had shone in the kitchen for years, but the kitchen eventually became her basket because it inhibited her from expressing another emergent dimension of herself.

The world of the kitchen can mean any man or woman's world that enabled the person's light to shine at one point in time but impedes it at another. The impediments that prevent us from moving into new worlds are cultural, familial, and personal. We learn from our families and society what it means to be real men or real women, good or bad citizens, religious or irreligious. This acculturation process challenges us to live out certain dimensions of our selves but it can also prevent us from developing to our full potentials. Feminists, for example, continually point out sexism in the workplace and the government. Religious institutions no less than secular ones have also helped keep people under baskets by restricting what women can do.

In *New World*, Martha and Mary's hospitality towards Jesus is superseded by his hospitality in inviting Mary to enter a world where her light could shine in a new way. It is also a standing invitation to all of us to explore new worlds of meaning in our own lives. We may not care to accept the invitation because it challenges us to redefine who we are. Fearing the loss of a light we already possess, we might prefer settling for safety rather than risk giving birth to the light we could become.

Can we recall those times when the light born of our risks made taking the risks well worth the venture?

OUR KIND

They came to Gerasene territory on the other side of the lake. As he got out of the boat, he was immediately met by a man from the tombs who had an unclean spirit. "What is your name," Jesus asked him. "Legion is my name," he answered. "There are hundreds of us."

Mark 5:1ff

"We've got to live with our own kind." Whenever Lem said this to Fanny and the kids, they knew they would repeat the familiar pattern of packing their belongings, selling their home, and relocating to a different part of the city.

"But Lem," Fanny pleaded, "I'm tired of moving. Why do you want to move this time?"

"Too many divorced people in the neighborhood," he answered. "They're a bad influence on the kids." Fanny shook her head sadly. The first time that Lem said he wanted to be with his own kind he was referring to his kind of skin color. "Too many of 'them' in the neighborhood," he whispered, pointing to a Latino walking down the street. "They have a strange way of talking. Not like us!" The second time he decided to be with his own kind he meant something else. "They don't make my kind of money," he confided to Fanny. "The value of our property is going down because their kind is moving in."

And now they were moving again. "This had better be the last time," Fanny warned. But it wasn't. Within the next year and a half they moved three more times, always because the people in the neighborhood were not Lem's kind. Their worship or politics or clubs weren't like his. They didn't dress or eat or dance as he did. Lem and his family moved to more and more exclusive sections of the city where Lem thought their kind lived. Finally, Fanny had had enough. She issued an ultimatum. "Lem, if you want to move, go ahead. But the kids and I are staying here. We've had it!"

"But, but...don't you want to be with our own kind?" Lem was shocked that Fanny could think otherwise.

"'Our kind'? Are you looney? We hardly have any friends left because you keep finding reasons why they're not really our kind. From now on find your own kind on your own because I've decided you're not *my* kind!"

"Well...if, if that's the way you want it," he sniffed, "I don't need your kind." A week later Lem moved out of the house into an apartment.

"I'll be fine, just fine," he thought as he looked out of his second-floor apartment window onto a neighborhood populated with folks he was certain were his own kind. After all, he had chosen it because the men there wore his kind of suits, they drove his kind of car, voted his kind of politics, and shopped in his kind of supermarket. "Ah, yes," he smiled, "I'm contented here. They're all like me. I think I'll take a little walk down the street."

Lem left his apartment and began his tour of the neighborhood. Humming "My Kind of Town," Lem hadn't walked more than two blocks when he found himself looking into the window of a liquor store. "Hmmm, I think I'll go in and get a bottle of scotch." Inside he scanned the shelves for his favorite brand. Becoming more and more agitated because he couldn't find his kind, Lem's face reddened and his eyes rolled back so that only the whites were visible. Turning on his heels, he faced the proprietor and screamed, "Where is our kind?"

Startled, the owner asked, "Our kind of what?"

"Where is our kind?" Lem shouted again.

"Sir, your kind of..."

"Where is our kind?" Again the same question but now the sound of Lem's voice was so ominous that frightened customers fled the store. Going berserk, Lem began clearing the shelves of all the bottles. "We want our kind!" he howled. The owner cowered behind the counter to avoid the flying bottles. The police soon arrived with a straitjacket and Lem was taken away to a distant place called The Tombs. The Tombs were dark caves near a cemetery on the outskirts of the city. There Lem didn't need to worry about living with other kinds of people because only his kind would ever dare to live there. And what kind was that?

"Our name is Legion!" the voices babbled. "But don't worry, you're our kind of guy! You think, act, and talk like us! Who could ask for anything more?" Lem knew the voices were right. And he was so weary that he just wished he could die. In fact several times he had attempted suicide by hurling himself against the jagged edges of rock near the opening to The Tombs.

"I'm sick of my kind," he cried. "It's a living hell—living only with my own kind. What can I do? Will no one help me?"

"Hey man, I will," a voice said softly.

"Wha...?" Lem spun around and spied a small, brown-skinned man leaning against a rock. Lem's eyes opened wide. What was this fellow doing here? He wasn't Lem's kind in any sense. He fell to his knees and blurted, "Jesus, Son of the Most High God! What do you want with our kind? Don't punish us!"

"Hey, man, don't get excited. Who do you think I am? My name is Jesús Jimenez. I'm jes' the gardener from the cemetery across the way. You used to live in our neighborhood. Remember? Then you pick up and leave one day, you and your family. Too bad—we was jes' getting to know you, man. What did you say your name was now?"

"Legion is our name! There are many of us but we're really all one of a kind. Please, please help me, Jesus!"

"Jesús, man, not Jesus," he said. "You're in bad shape, man." Jesús knelt down, placed his arm around Lem and gently rocked him in his arms for a minute. "It's not so bad now, is it?" he said. His voice was soothing, but Lem's body was still shaking. Jesús asked, "Do you wanna stay with me and my family for a while? We got a spare room."

"With you? You? Jes...I mean Jesús?"

"Yeah!"

"Oh, yes! Yes! Jesús! Jesús!"

No sooner had he said, "Yes, Jesús," than his body quieted down while in a nearby field a herd of pigs was going wild.

Jesús laughed. "I guess they got their own kind of problems....looks like a pig race!" Lem smiled at Jesús. He was beginning to find his kind of people.

REFLECTION

When we think of "exclusive" neighborhoods, are we offended? Maybe not. We have heard "exclusive" used so often in relation to beautiful suburbs with expensive homes, perfectly manicured lawns and gardens, BMWs, Cadillacs, Lincoln Continentals, well-heeled and well-dressed people that we may never reflect on the meaning of the word itself. Exclusive comes from the Latin *ex claudere*, which means to shut out, reject. *Our Kind* live in exclusive neighborhoods and "any other kind" is shut out, rejected.

Of course, the people who live in these neighborhoods don't ordinarily exert any physical force to shut out "the other kind." But they probably assume that whoever comes into their neighborhood had better be able to keep up with their Joneses (if they know what is good for them). Living in an exclusive neighborhood or associating exclusively with certain kinds of people encapsulates us in a very small world. It keeps us under the basket, shielding us from people who have different ideas, tastes, aspirations, and problems. Finally, our passion to be exclusive becomes an affliction. It leads us to reject whatever is different and alien within ourselves. We are afraid of the "inner stranger" who doesn't speak our language, think our thoughts, or share our feelings—but who preys upon us in our moods, our strange desires, impulses, dreams, and obsessions. We are left with our demons, and they are many.

And how can we be saved? By being inclusive. Jesus is the brown-skinned alien who includes, draws in, embraces, and is finally included in Lem's life. To be inclusive is to invite others into our lives. It is to own our inner stranger—our shadow, as Jung named it. We are inclusive when our kind is hospitable toward every other kind.

Are we porchlights welcoming only a select few into our lives? Or are our lights burning brightly for people coming from all walks of life? Could something as simple as driving our car in neighborhoods we rarely if ever visit be our first step in becoming the porchlight, the sign that all visitors are welcome at our front door?

BROKEN PROMISE

On that same day two of Jesus' followers were making their way to a village named Emmaus seven miles distant from Jerusalem, discussing as they went all that had happened. Luke 24:13-14

"Life is a broken promise now that Jesus is dead," Cleo complained to his friend Eli as they walked on the road to Emmaus. "What's there to live for? Now everything has fallen apart." Twenty-five years earlier, Cleo had had such high hopes. "My future's promising," he had boasted. "It's looking great! I'm going to find me a good-looking gal. We'll get married, settle down, and have bright kids who'll really go places. And I'll own a business that will make me a mint." A promising future? That's what he thought twenty-five years ago. But now, at age forty-five, it was a different story.

Cleo had gotten married but not to the girl of his dreams. True, she had pale blue eyes, ruby lips, and a winning smile but she also had a nose bent just slightly to the left. She cooked a good meal but she couldn't sew a button on a shirt if her life depended on it. She had a good ear for listening but she wasn't much for talking. Humming was her long suit but she sang with a twang.

As for their marriage, sometimes they'd chirp along but just as often they'd growl. Smiling one day, they snarled the next. All in all, the marriage wasn't bad but Cleo had had such high hopes—and now life seemed a broken promise.

And his children? The kids who'd eagerly listen to mom and dad's words of wisdom? The bright kids who were really going places? One was smart in math but dumb in spelling; the other was smart in spelling but dumb in math. They weren't bad looking but they had their mother's nose which bent just slightly to the left. As for listening to their parents' words of advice, they listened, all right. Then they'd scratch their heads, shrug their shoulders, and do whatever they wanted. Both of them moved to the other side of town and worked in the local glue factory. It didn't take much to make them happy. But Cleo had had such high hopes for them and now life seemed a broken promise.

And the promising career? Cleo owned and operated a bagel bakery. Not the smallest business in town but not the biggest. His bagels weren't bad but they weren't the best either. He made money but not the mint he said he'd make. All in all, his was a modestly successful business. But Cleo had had such high hopes and now life was passing by. It seemed a broken promise.

As if to prove that "There's no fool like an old fool," Cleo got suckered in again when he was well into his forties. This time he pinned his high hopes on Jesus of Nazareth. "Surely he won't let me down," Cleo thought. "Jesus is the one. He's the wave of the future. He's our promise. A real winner! His power base is here and he's going to drive the bully boys away. He'll make this a land of promise again and we'll be on the move." But the promised one was nailed to the tree and left to die a broken man, hardly a winner and no one's future. Just another broken promise. And for Cleo, the last straw.

"I just don't understand," Cleo complained as he and his friend Eli walked the dusty road to Emmaus. "What went wrong? He wasn't supposed to die. That wasn't in the cards.

Where's the winner we were promised? I'll tell you...nowhere! Sure, a couple of women report he's alive but that's absurd, impossible!"

"May I join you?"

"Wha...?" Cleo and Eli turned to see a man walking a few feet behind.

"May I join you? I don't like walking this road alone."

"Suit yourself," Cleo said. "We were just talking about Jesus of Nazareth."

"Oh? What about him?"

"You mean you haven't heard the news?"

"I've been away for three days."

"Well, he's not what we'd thought. Just another flash in the pan, another broken promise." And Cleo proceeded to tell the man all that had happened not only to Jesus, but all the disappointments in his own life as well.

"Hmmm," the man stroked his chin. "Your story sounds vaguely familiar. About three years ago I was convinced that all of us—my friends, the people I talked to, myself—that we all had a promising future. Changes in our lives were to take place over night. The day would dawn when people from all over would sit around one table and enjoy each other's company. We knew we'd have to overcome certain obstacles. But we'd win out! We'd triumph! Life seemed so promising!" The stranger paused.

"And?" Cleo waved a hand.

"Well...not everyone shared our enthusiasm. In fact, some people were downright hostile. Even the friends we counted on most betrayed us." His voice grew raspy. "And worst of all, the one whose support and love I relied on most seemed to have abandoned me when I needed him most!"

"Really?" Both Cleo and Eli's eyes widened.

"Yes, when I was just hanging there, hurting, I said, 'Where are you when I need you?' And, you know, he said nothing. Nothing!"

"No kidding! So what did you do?" Eli asked.

"At first I thought, 'That's it! There goes the future! Promises, promises! Right out the window!' I felt wretched and in a lot of pain. But then I thought, 'So there's a change of plans. So it's not working out according to my expectations! I can't do anything about that. I'll just hang in there, wait, and trust it will all work out. What else can I do?'"

"And what happened?"

"I think I died."

"I know the feeling well," Cleo sighed.

"You what?" Eli was all in a muddle.

"I think I died," the stranger repeated, looking off into the distance.

"But...you're here. How...?"

"I'm here but...all I know is that the one I thought had abandoned me pulled me through. And now I'm alive in a new way. Even my friends aren't going to recognize me right away. It's a changed ball game, believe me! Just when you think 'It's over. My life is just a heap of broken promises...' Surprise! Back alive in a way no one expected!"

"Hmmm, I never thought of it that way," Cleo said. Turning to the man he asked, "Have we met before? Your voice...your smile..."

"Maybe I resemble someone you know."

"Could be. Could be," Cleo said, trying without success to recall who this engaging young man resembled. However, they had reached Emmaus and the stranger told them he had to continue on his way. But Cleo and Eli persuaded him to join them for a light lunch.

When they arrived, Cleo spread a white tablecloth over a workbench and placed a small loaf of bread, a carafe of wine, and three goblets on it. Once they sat down, Cleo invited the stranger to do the honor of breaking the bread. Taking the bread into his hands, the man ran his fingers over the small loaf. "Nice texture! Did you bake it?"

"Yes," Cleo answered. "This morning."

"Ah, freshly risen," he whispered, "and it smells so good."

No sooner had the stranger spoken the word "risen" than Cleo's heart began beating faster. He remembered the stranger's words about coming alive in a new way and it struck Cleo how closely this man's experience paralleled Jesus'—his hopes, his betrayal, his death, and now? Both Cleo and Eli's eyes were riveted on their guest as he broke the bread and shared the cup. When they had finished the meal the man said, "We know each other better now, don't we? I hope you will remember me whenever you break bread together."

"Yes," Cleo said softly. "We will."

The stranger rose. "It's time for me to go. I have much to do. I have many friends with whom I'll be breaking bread. Thank you for your hospitality. Please stay sitting. I'll let myself out." And the man left the house.

"It's him," Cleo whispered.

"I know," Eli said.

Cleo rose, went to the window, and watched the stranger as he disappeared over the horizon. "He's come back, Eli. He's come back!"

REFLECTION

"Hangin' in there" expresses how we are getting along: how we're handling a job, working through a relationship, doing in school. For some of us, hangin' in there is not particularly difficult. We're pretty confident that we'll do all right; we'll manage. However, for others, hangin' in there means being painfully helpless. We're not really sure if we'll survive a difficult time: a midlife transition or the loss of a loved one. The pain of just hangin' in there can reveal just how broken we are in body, mind, and spirit.

The times of just hangin' in there are frequently dark and depressing, hardly times we'd expect to experience any light.

Yet, as our story suggests, hangin' in there can also mean trusting and waiting. We wait and wait. For what? For something new to develop. For a break through brokenness. For transformation. For new life.

Trusting and waiting doesn't mean that after a period of hangin' in there we finally figure a way out. It means we have reached an impasse and cannot find any way to stop hangin' in there. All we can do is trust that there is One who is with us as we hang and that, as in Jesus' hanging and dying, this One will be with us.

Hangin' in there, then, is both a sign of our helplessness and the medium through which we can experience transformation from death to life, not because this has to happen but because we believe that the One who raised Jesus from the dead has promised it will happen.

As the medium of transformation, hangin' in there is paradoxically darkness and light: It is a blinding light. We do not see a way out of our predicament and, because we are blind, we wait in the dark to "see" in a new way. Is waiting itself the first necessary step we need to take to experience light in a new way?

THE TOPBANANA TREE

Now the serpent was the most cunning of all the animals that the LORD God had made. The serpent asked the woman, "Did God really tell you not to eat from any of the trees in the garden?"

Genesis 3:1

"Either she's not gotten around to getting her wardrobe or she's so naïve it hasn't occurred to her that she needs one," Mr. S wisecracked to himself as he spied on Eve from behind one of the many green bushes in the garden. "I'll wager she is naïve. She doesn't seem the least bit embarrassed sitting there sipping tea, naked as a newborn babe except for that silly garden hat she's wearing," he observed. "Hmmmm....I'll bet Mr. G would like to keep her an infant, too. It would be far too messy for him if she and her husband woke up from their dream of innocence. Then he'd really have his hands full."

"For starters, she'd want a wardrobe. That would lead to agonizing over what to buy, getting Adam upset over her spending sprees, being dissatisfied with what she'd bought, going out to purchase more clothes, complaining to Mr. G about her problems, blah, blah, blah! Yes, he'd like to keep matters simple. But I for one don't think that's fair. Why should she have it so easy, enjoying life without any questions or doubts, while I find life so complicated? I think I'll pay her

91

a little visit." Mr. S slunk over to Eve's garden table where she was nibbling on a chocolate chip cookie. Tipping his straw hat, he asked "Ssssay, would you mind a little company?"

Not startled in the least, Eve smiled and said, "Oh, no, not at all. Could I fix you some tea, Mr....ah?"

"Mr. S," he whispered seductively. "I happen to be a neighbor. And, yes, I would like a cup." As Eve prepared the tea with just a little sugar, he continued, "What a sssplendid sssanctuary you have here."

"Thank you. My husband and I think it's a bit of heaven on earth."

"Sssss," Mr. S hissed as his face contorted at the word "heaven." Then regaining his composure he gushed enthusiastically, "Those are mighty nice fruit trees. The fruit looks sssimply sssumptuous! I bet you've sssampled them all?"

"Not quite," she answered. Rising to her full height, the graceful curves of her body now highlighted in the morning sun, she pointed to a tree at a spot where the inscription "Middle of the Garden" was carved on a marble slab. "Mr. G told us we may not eat the fruit of that tree," she dutifully observed.

"Wha...?" Worldly wise as he was, even Mr. S blushed as she stood there, completely unaware that being naked had implications for onlookers.

"Why are you looking at *me*?" she asked innocently. "The *tree* is over there."

Perspiring, Mr. S murmured, "Oh yesss, yesss, over there," as he strove to focus on the one tree whose fruit the couple were ordered never to eat. "Why that's the Topbanana tree!" he noted approvingly. "Topbanana sends me up a tree. It's marvelous!"

"Topbanana?" That was a new name to Eve. "Mr. G never mentioned its name. Only that we had better not eat it if we didn't want to become topa...topa?"

"Topbananas."

"Yes. Topbananas."

"Really? Becoming topbananas? What's so bad about that? I'm surprised at Mr. G," he exclaimed, affecting a disappointing tone. "I never dreamed Mr. G would forbid anyone from eating topbananas."

"Why?" Eve's curiosity was aroused.

"Well, confidentially, Eve..." Sliding a finger slowly down Eve's back, Mr. S continued in a hushed voice, "Topbanana has got twice as many vitamins as other fruit. It's high in potassium and iron, low in cholesterol, reduces chances for cancer, heart failure, arthritis and lung disease, takes care of irregularity, and..." he paused as he prepared himself to deliver the winning line, "...just one bite of a topbanana will put you in complete control of your life."

"Gee, does it really do all that?" Eve marveled.

"Most certainly," he reassured her, dancing the fingers of his right hand on the nape of her neck.

"But Mr. G said we'd die if we ate it."

"Die? Oh never, never. You solve all your problems with sssucculent, sssavory topbananasss. You wouldn't need anything or anybody to tell you how to run your life. Yes, you'd really be topbanana. In fact, you'd be able to tell others what to do."

"Wow! We'd become like, like....Mr. G!" Eve did a spritely dance over to the tree in the middle of the garden and fell on her knees. "To think it would take care of irregularity! Adam would like that. He hasn't been himself lately. If topbanana is all that you say it is, then Adam and I would be pretty much on our own. I'm fond of Mr. G but...," she paused, then added resentfully, "it unnerves Adam and me to have someone always telling us what's good and what's bad for us."

Eve could no longer contain herself. She rose and plucked a topbanana while Mr. S looked on triumphantly. "Good, good, go ahead! You'll love it!" he urged.

Eve sank her teeth into the fruit. "Phew! Really bitter!" Her lips puckered up. "It looks better than it tastes. I hope there's no aftertaste."

"Oh, no, no," Mr. S assured her, crossing his fingers behind his back.

At that moment Adam appeared from the other end of the garden. "What are you doing?"

"I'm eating a topbanana, Adam."

"Topbanana?"

"Yes, it's the fruit Mr. G told us never to eat."

"What?" he cried.

"Oh, don't worry, dear! This gentleman, Mr. S, has been enlightening me about its value. One bite and you're in charge of your life. It's your show and you call the shots. You're topbanana all the way."

"Really?" Adam's eyes widened.

Eve strolled over to Adam and dangled the fruit in front of him. "What's more," she whispered confidentially, "it will take care of your irregularity."

That did it! He devoured it greedily, though his face registered the same sour displeasure.

"I know, I know. It's bitter. But Mr. S assures us there's no aftertaste."

"Ha! Ha! Ha!" Mr. S laughed ominously. "No aftertaste! Ha! Ha! Ha! Wait and see if there's no aftertaste!"

"What are you laughing at, Mr. S?" Eve puzzled.

"Look at yourselves!" he sneered.

"Adam, turn around! Don't look at me," Eve pleaded as she attempted to cover her whole body with her hands. Since this was impossible, Eve ran off to find anything available to hide her nakedness. Adam stood there dumbfounded.

"Ha! Ha!" Mr. S pointed to Adam's body. Adam's face flushed. "What's the matter? Do you find me inadequate somehow?" he asked defensively.

Mr. S rubbed his hands together. "Now I know you've digested the topbanana. Your question sssmacks of the ssour aftertaste you and your sssons will always know. You'll never feel adequate again. Ever!" he shouted. Abruptly, he resumed a chatty tone. "Well, I have to be on my way. I'm sure we will be seeing one another again, Adam." He slithered into the foliage as Adam puzzled over what Mr. S meant about the aftertaste. Adam began to feel more and more uneasy. Moments earlier the garden had been home, but now it appeared strange and ominous. He wanted to run away but every direction he turned seemed equally hostile.

Spotting a vine climbing a nearby tree, he grabbed several of its shoots, tied them together and draped them over his body. No sooner had Adam finished than he spied Eve several feet away. She had covered herself similarly. For a moment they stared at one another, two persons not only aliens on their own land, but also to one another.

"Adam?" Eve called softly as if she were speaking a stranger's name.

"Eve?" He found her name foreign, too.

Warily, as if meeting for the first time, they inched towards one another until they were standing face to face. There was an awkward silence. Finally, Adam spoke. "Why, why did you make me eat the topbanana?"

"*Make* you eat? I didn't *make* you do anything," Eve said, folding her arms, ready to stand her ground.

"You practically shoved it down my throat," Adam persisted.

"I did *not*! Mr. S was behind it all. He kept telling me how great it was."

"Oh come on...don't pass the buck! I..." Adam stopped, waited, and checked himself, sensing things were escalating into a huge argument. "See what's happening? We're arguing and acting horribly. I thought the topbanana was supposed to do away with all our problems. We..."

"It will! It will! We'll manage! We'll call the shots...oh...." Eve remembered promising Adam that eating the fruit would enable them to "call the shots." *Then* the words seemed liberating; *now* they appeared to be charged with responsibility.

"We can manage?" Adam laughed bitterly. "If Mr. S is correct, I for one am never going to feel adequate again. I'll be trying forever to prove I'm adequate. Isn't that what being topbanana is all about?" Then, looking directly into Eve's eyes, he continued somberly, "We're on our own, all right! But I'm not sure this is what we had in mind."

"What are we going to do, Adam?" Eve asked fearfully.

"What are we going to do?" Adam repeated slowly. "We're supposed to know the answer, aren't we?" He paused and continued, "And all we really know is just how helpless we are without Mr. G. What do you say we go and share that bit of knowledge with him? And let him do what we could never do—save us!"

REFLECTION

Are we satisfied to participate in the light or do we want to *be* the Light? There is a considerable difference between the two. This becomes apparent if we think of people who get carried away by "light" inflation. For example, a football team wins and the team members, cheerleaders, and fans all shout, "We're Number One! We're the best!" Or we get a Ph.D. in Philosophy and lay claim to being The Philosopher. The expression "A little knowledge is a dangerous thing" implies "light inflation" and all the problems it presents. We know a little, but get inflated and think we know everything. We are all light and in us there is no darkness. We think we can make no mistakes, do no wrong, and never get hurt.

But these illusions are generated by light inflation. We aren't really the Light. We discover one day, through an accident or an egregious error or a bad choice that we are not pure Light but contain quite a bit of darkness. If we are lucky, we might also be ready to call upon the One who is Light to save us from any future light-headed illusions.

Were there times when we felt giddy about our accomplishments? Did we ever think we had it made and could do no wrong? That we certainly knew more about whatever than the people around us? And how did this influence our behavior toward others?

NARROW DOOR

He went through cities and towns teaching—all the while making his way toward Jerusalem. Someone asked him, "Lord, are they few in number who are to be saved?" He replied: "Try to come in through the narrow door. Many, I tell you, will try to enter and be unable." Luke 13:22-24

"It appeared in *Haute Couture!*"

"And *Entre Nous!*"

"Not to mention *Pour Nous Seulement!*"

Sipping herbal tea in Mildred's sitting room, the three women were breathless. And why? Each had read in their exclusive magazines about the elegant party the king was going to host at the palace the following month. "It's obvious to me," Mildred sniffed, "that not just anybody is getting in through the palace doors that night."

"Of course not," Marcella agreed. "Otherwise why would the announcement have appeared in our magazines? Who but our kind gets *Haute Couture* or *Entre Nous?*"

"Not to mention *Pour Nous Seulement*," Marlena mewed. "Besides, the announcement clearly states that any of us who wants to attend should submit our names to the arrangements committee. What else could that mean except that the arrangements committee is actually a screening committee?"

"And that our kind of people are the only kind who will get through the palace doors," Mildred assured them. "Which means those who have our kind of color: skin, hair, and eyes; who practice our kind of religion: sweet-shepherd-Jesus-of the-sweet-talking sheep; and, of course, the kind of people who live in our kind of homes on our side of town and who wouldn't think of receiving third-class mail in their boxes."

"As well as those who love in our kind of way...which is loving our kind of people," Marcella instructed. Folding her hands, eyes lifted, she whispered, "And who share our ambition to insure more and more blessings for our kind."

Mildred raised a finger and purred, "Yes indeedy, very few are going to get through the palace doors! I'm going to write to the screening committee right away and let them know that Marvin and I are available. I'll let them know we're the kind of people they're looking for."

"Well, Melvin and I certainly know we're two of the right kind," Marlena huffed, "and we thank each other and God for that every night!"

"Girls," Mildred announced, "I'm ready to write to the committee that I am in complete agreement with their policy of being very selective. What kind of an example would we be giving our children if we let every thrill-seeking Tom, Dick, and Harry through the door? Hummph!" Mildred rose to her feet and declared, "Let's write our letters!" The others nodded and each went home to write to the committee.

The letters they produced contained complete profiles of themselves and their husbands: country clubs, credit cards, expensive restaurants, department stores, and banks they frequented; important people they knew; schools their children attended. Satisfied they had sufficiently informed the committee of their virtues and that they deserved an escort through the palace doors, they sent their letters to the palace.

Within a couple of days each received an invitation to the party. They were ecstatic! Obviously the committee was impressed with their credentials because the invitation read,

"The king is especially delighted to have your kind of person at our party." The invitation confirmed everything they had discussed earlier in the week.

The night of the party the women wore evening gowns purchased from the *Our Kind of Gown* boutique. Their husbands, Melvin, Mervin, and Marvin, were also dressed to kill. The three couples stepped out of their plush homes and got into their chauffeur-driven limos. They formed a mini-caravan passing through the streets of their far, far eastern suburban neighborhood, populated exclusively with their kind of people: skin, hair, eyes—and cash. Finally, they reached the magnificent palace doors. "Ah! We've arrived," they chortled and then broke into a chorus of, "The king is my kind of guy...the king is my kind of guy..." But their good humor turned to horror at what they saw when they stepped out of their limos and looked toward the ancient portals.

People had driven up in old jalopies, Pintos, Vegas, and other bug-size cars; some had come on bikes, trikes, motorcycles and rickshaws. A few even came on mules and horses, while a long assortment of bag ladies were pushing shopping carts toward the doors. And the people! They were white, black, yellow, red, spotted, and striped. Dressed in bib overalls, granny dresses, miniskirts, caftans, dhotis, or wearing shawls, boas, babushkas, beads on their heads, they all marched proudly toward the large palace doors. About the only thing they had in common was the post card that they presented to the doorkeepers.

"I don't understand," Mildred protested. "How can *they* get in? Surely they didn't go through the screening committee! How could they? They don't have special invitations like we do! Doorkeeper, what is going on?"

"Ma'am, the king sent out invitations on post cards to everyone in the realm. See!" The doorkeeper showed Mildred a post card on which the invitation was printed. It was worded exactly the same way as hers: "The king is especially delighted to have your kind of person at our party." The doorkeeper continued, "Well, you know what happens to third-class mail. Sometimes people just ignore it. So, after the post cards had been sent, the king decided to publish the announcement in a few magazines and requested that anyone who wrote to his arrangements committee be given an invitation. That is the kind of invitation you are holding."

"But...but, the king is letting in people who aren't our kind!"

"Our kind? I'm sorry I don't understand what you mean," the doorkeeper answered. "Are you coming in?" he asked.

The three couples wailed in unison, "But they're not our kind! They're not our kind! How can we go in when they're not our kind?!"

By now people were streaming in from the inner city, the countryside, the suburbs, the farms. In order to accommodate the crush, the doorkeepers opened the huge palace doors even wider and admitted the guests without requiring them to show their post cards.

From outside it was possible to see into the grand ballroom. Everyone inside was dancing, singing, feasting, and enjoying one another. The king stood in the middle of it all, laughing and kicking up a storm! Still Mildred, Marlena, and Marcella and their husbands, Melvin, Marvin, and Mervin, chanted, "We can't go in! We can't go in! Not with any other kind but our kind!" Pounding their fists, they refused to go through the doors either because they didn't want to go in or because it had now become impossible. Had they locked themselves out?

One thing was very evident that night: They were truly spending the evening with their kind of people!

REFLECTION

Some people's understanding of being special is being superior to, and therefore better than, everyone else. As a game it is known as One Up.

One Up can be inoffensive. If we say to a friend that we caught a fish twelve inches long and, winking mischievously, our friend says that he caught one fifteen inches long, our friend is one up. Or if we say that all of our brothers and sisters graduated from college and our friend says all his graduated with honors, our friend is again one up. However, if we quickly add that the members of our family went to Yale when we know our friend's family all went to Dogpatch U., then *we* are one up. The game becomes nasty when we tell our friend that our mother makes great meatloaf because she doesn't use cheap meat like some mothers we know. That is being one up by cruelly putting down another. It's a more serious thing when we find it necessary to put down another's point of view, eating habits, dress habits, religious convictions, etc., in order to be one up. Played that way, the game creates division. Why, then, do we play it?

Are we are afraid of losing our individuality, that which makes us who we are? If we are no different from others, then who are we? What is our worth? Our value? Instead of establishing our uniqueness, playing the game of One Up turns us into PODs—Possessive, Offensive, and Defensive. PODs are dependent on what they own for self-definition, so they become increasingly possessive. They attack the integrity of others and grow offensive. They think others are out to get them (just like they are out to get everyone else), and this makes them defensive.

How do we ever stop playing One Up? How can we escape the destiny of a POD? It only stops once we realize that being unique doesn't mean being completely independent from others, and then acknowledge our interdependence. We are most ourselves when we relate to others in ways that emphasize our mutuality. A model is beautiful because there is someone to admire her. What is a doctor without a trusting patient, or a teacher without an interested student, or a preacher without a receptive congregation?

Letting the light shine doesn't mean outshining others as much as highlighting and being highlighted by others as in a colorful rainbow of light. Attempting to outshine others is just another way we hide the fact that we are still in some ways possessive, offensive, and defensive—PODs, not persons of light.

Do we understand that we stand to gain by acknowledging our interdependence with all of creation? Do we realize we risk losing everything if we insist on establishing our light as the only light?

DADDY

"A man had two sons. The younger of them said to his father, 'Father, give me the share of the estate that is coming to me.' So the father divided up the property." Luke 15:11ff

"Junior, you've done it again! Putting Ex-lax in the chocolate chip cookie batter for Ms. Purdy's baking class. What am I going to do with you? Your brother Ralph never did that. He's responsible. Tell me, son, how much Ex-lax did you use? And did they have to call off classes?"

"Junior, you owe Rev. Duffy an apology. He was kind enough to visit and give us Sunday school literature. Why'd you drop the water balloon on his head from your bedroom window? Your brother Ralph wouldn't do that. He's responsible. What I'd like to know is...what was the expression on the Reverend's face when he got drenched?"

"Junior, how many times have I told you I don't want any egg throwing contests in or out of the coop! It puts the chickens off schedule for a week. I never saw your brother Ralph and his friends do that. He's responsible. Just the same, who hit the target most?"

"Momma, I don't know what we're going to do with that boy," Daddy pondered as he brought the cup of coffee to his lips at the breakfast table. "He's a hellraiser!" he added with thinly veiled praise.

"Mmmm." Momma studied Daddy's face carefully as he shook his head over Junior's latest caper. She was more interested in how Daddy would handle it than with the incident itself.

"Imagine, running off with the girls' clothes while they were skinnydipping in the river," he muttered with feigned indignation.

"Yes, imagine...," Momma repeated, not taking her eyes off Daddy.

Leaning back in his chair, he sighed, "My goodness, that must have been some sight...ten girls trying to decide which one would scramble up the tree to get their clothes back." Barely disguising his admiration, he added, "And with Junior watching from the top of the tree!"

"Sounds like you wish you had been there," Momma remarked as she took another sip of coffee.

Too quickly dismissing her observation he protested, "Oh, no, no, Momma. I simply want to get a clear picture in my mind of exactly what happened so I can deal with the situation. What Junior did was wrong. He'll have to be punished. We don't want to put up with any of that nonsense again."

"Just like we punished him in the past?" Momma's voice had a touch of skepticism.

"This time it'll be different! You'll see, Momma," he tried to assure her by shaking his finger, indicating he meant business. "He's got to learn to be responsible...like his brother. Ralph never did anything like that when he was Junior's age. He was careful and didn't need us to look after him. In fact, he was so quiet we didn't even notice him half the time." Daddy sat up straight in his chair as he continued his assessment of his older son's character.

"He's a hard worker," Momma added.

"And serious," Daddy contributed. "Maybe too serious," he mumbled.

"What was that?"

"Nothing, nothing." Daddy didn't care to pursue the matter further. He admired Ralph's business acumen, work habits, and his sense of filial duty. Moreover, he had routinely praised Ralph as a model of responsibility to his younger son, especially when Junior acted irresponsibly. Daddy wondered if that was a mistake. Hadn't Ralph repeatedly told him, "You expect too much from me," and didn't Junior suffer by comparison? Yes, maybe that was why he didn't care to think too deeply about his relationship with his sons. He was pained to realize how unjust he had been toward both of them.

"So, what are you going to do this time that will be different? What kind of punishment do you have in mind?" Momma inquired.

"I realize now I was too harsh on Junior. So..."

"Too harsh?" Momma interrupted. She couldn't believe he meant what he said.

"By always comparing him with Ralph," he tried to explain.

"By simply mentioning Ralph's sense of responsibility and then immediately doting on Junior, asking all about his exploits? And you think you've been too harsh on him? Who are you trying to fool?" Momma's face was flushed.

"Who am I trying to fool?" Daddy was taken off guard. "I'm not trying to fool anyone," he protested.

"No?" Momma continued the offensive. "You just might be trying to fool yourself!"

"What do you mean? Why would I want to fool myself?"

Just then the kitchen door swung open, and there was Junior. Smiling with a conspicuous innocence, he strutted into the room and grabbed a handful of cookies from the cookie jar. "Hi, Momma. Hi, Daddy."

"Sit down, Junior," Daddy ordered in a manner that signaled to Momma he was taking the matter very seriously. However, Junior chose to stand and Momma was not impressed. Embarrassed, Daddy continued, "I've been wanting to talk to you about that incident at the river...I..."

"Daddy, I'm sorry about that. It was dumb of me to do a thing like that," Junior confessed with less than total candor.

"You are?" Daddy was both relieved and surprised.

"Yeah, but I've got something else that's on my mind. Daddy, I'm leaving here. I've gotta split!"

"You what?!" Momma and Daddy stood up simultaneously.

Admiring himself in one of the well-scrubbed pots hanging over the kitchen sink, he addressed his reflection, "It's time for me to move on. I've been raisin' a lot of hell around here, and I think I can fare better somewhere else." He didn't sound very remorseful.

"Junior," Daddy pleaded, "maybe we can talk. I've been thinking. Maybe I've been too harsh on you. What are we going to do if you leave? You're our son!"

Junior turned to face Daddy. "No need to worry, Daddy, Ralph is here."

"I don't care if he is here, Junior, you're my son. I love you. I want a son here I can love. I..."

"Daddy!" Momma was horrified.

"I didn't mean that..." Daddy replied weakly as he slumped back into his chair.

"Daddy," Junior came to the point, oblivious of Daddy's confession, "I need money. I need plenty of money. I want my inheritance now!"

Tears filled his father's eyes. "My sons, my sons!" he cried. "Yes, yes, they are both my sons and I will divide the inheritance between them. I will treat them equally. But, Junior," and here Daddy reached out to embrace him, "you I love."

"And I love you too, Daddy," Junior said matter-of-factly as he gave Daddy a quick hug, "but I gotta go. And I don't have any more time to talk about it. You'll be OK. Ralph will be around." Junior walked to the door, opened it, winked at both of them and said, "After all, he's so responsible." The door slammed shut.

"He's so responsible," Daddy repeated slowly, "he's so hard-working and honest. I admire him but, but..."

"But what?" Momma asked gently.

"But the son I love is leaving. And I don't know what to do."

"You'll have to settle for a son you admire and respect," Momma concluded as she got up and began gathering the breakfast dishes.

And indeed there was nothing he could do except hope for the return of the son he loved and continue to respect the one who remained at home.

REFLECTION

In a day when so many parents would love to see their grown children finally leave home, we can ask why Daddy hated to see his son take off for a foreign country. Would he have felt equally bad if his older son had gone instead of the younger? The question becomes more interesting if we look at it in terms of our theme of light.

Did the father dote on his youngest son because he rejoiced in his son's light or did he delight in him because his son bodied forth his own light in ways that he had never been able to live out? Daddy seemed to take a vicarious pleasure in hearing his son's exploits. He seemed to experience some unlived dimensions of himself coming to light in his son's life. When Junior decided to leave home, was Daddy grieving for Junior, or was he grieving because his sole medium for letting his own light shine would no longer be available? His older son had the fortune or misfortune of not being the vehicle of light the younger son was. Perhaps he had been more like his father had always been: sober, responsible, businesslike. If that were the case, he was dispensable, but Junior, who was Daddy's unlived light, was not.

We don't know what happened to Daddy between Junior's leaving home and his return. Possibly, the old man was able to live out for himself his playful, childlike side that he had never done while Junior was at home. Possibly, but we aren't certain. We do know that as many overly serious men mature, they are called to integrate their neglected, playful side. Wisdom comes from accepting the old and the young in ourselves.

"Old Boy" is the designation for the Chinese sage Lao-tzu to whom the classic, the *Tao Te Ching*, is attributed. Only with Junior gone could Daddy's light side shine in full splendor. Only then could he love Junior in his own light and not as an extension of himself.

Are there times in our lives when we have to "let go" of others if we and they are to discover whose light belongs to whom? Painful as this letting go is, it might be the first step we take in letting be—letting each other's light shine in each one's own unique way.

THE PARTY

*As he moved on, Jesus saw a man named Matthew at his post where
taxes were collected. He said to him, "Follow me." Matthew got up
and followed him.* Matthew 9:9ff

"Parties? The last thing I want is a party. They're a waste of
time and you can't make money at a party." That's how Matt
responded to any suggestion of a celebration. His distaste for
parties was no recent acquisition. As a youngster he learned
this attitude from his parents.

"We don't believe in parties!" That's what they told him
when he asked if he could have a birthday party like his
friends. "Parties cost too much. Besides, you should spend
your time doing something profitable!"

"Like what?"

"Like making money."

Matt felt cheated. He wished that he could be special at
least one day of the year like the other kids. Their birthdays
were times for presents, balloons, paper hats, colorful plates
and napkins. But his birthday was just another day. And he
was ashamed when his friends asked why his parents never
gave him a party.

As the years passed, he learned to hide his hurt on birthdays by reminding himself of his parents' counsel: the value

of thrift and the wastefulness of parties. Of course, he made
certain to remember their advice on all the other special days
his parents didn't celebrate: holy days, national holidays,
graduations. Clearly, the lesson he learned was that nothing
in life was worth celebrating. And since he didn't celebrate
anything in his life, he decided not to celebrate anything in
anyone else's life either. All parties were out! Better to concen-
trate on doing what he had been told to do repeatedly by his
parents: make money.

And when he grew up? Well, at age twenty-four he got a
job that paid well, all right! But it wasn't the kind of job his
folks had in mind. He became a tax collector—a profession
that horrified them and made him a traitor in the eyes of others.

"How can you work for the Romans? Robbing *us* to fill *their*
pockets and your own?"

"I'm making money. Isn't that what you wanted?"

"But no one will want you in their company. You won't be
invited to their homes. You..."

"So what? Since when is being with others so important? I
don't need them!"

What his parents didn't realize was how relieved Matt felt
that he had become a hated tax collector. Now his isolation
wouldn't feel so personal. Now he was alone because of his
job, not because he was Matt. But in a strange way the attention Matt got as a tax collector met a need that his parents had
never met. Matt collected tolls on the border between Capernaum and Bethsaida and people had to notice him as he deter-
mined how much they owed on goods they were transport-
ing. Since he was an obstacle they couldn't ignore, he became
at least for a few moments the center of someone's attention.
Of course, he never would have admitted this need to himself.
He thought he was simply doing what was expected of any
good tax collector.

He sat at his desk day after day interrogating the travelers
who came through his doors. One day a young man entered

his office, sat down, and declared the few items he had to carry over the border. Matt made his computations and concluded, "That will cost fifteen dollars."

"Fifteen dollars? But I don't have fifteen."

"Then you can't cross the border."

"But I must!"

"Fork over the money or forget about your little trip!"

"Well, I don't have the money. But I do have food."

"Food. For what?"

"For a party." The man smiled broadly.

"A party? You must be crazy!"

"Don't you like parties? Haven't you ever had one?"

"Well...I...I...no, I've never had a party," Matt stammered, "and I don't intend..."

"You've never had a party? Well, Matt, it's time you had one; we'll throw it in your honor. It'll be a birthday bash!" he laughed.

"But...how do you know my name? And...it's not my birth..." Matt stopped, brought both hands to his mouth and said, "My God, today *is* my birthday! How...how...?"

"It doesn't matter how I know. What matters is you deserve a party! And you're going to get one." Before Matt knew what was happening the man had taken a white tablecloth from his knapsack, cleared the money table, and spread the tablecloth on the desk. Then he leaned out the window and cried to his friends, "Fellas! In here!" Four other young men entered the room. Their arms were loaded with cheese, fruit, wine, salami, and bagels. One of the men had balloons and streamers that he promptly strung from the beams.

Matt was too dumbfounded to protest. "I don't believe this," he murmured. Nor did the other travelers who crammed Matt's little office to pay their taxes.

"What's going on here?" they asked.

"Matt's party! Come and join us," the young man answered. "OK, Matt?"

"Why, why, yes," Matt answered. "I guess it is."

"But what about the tolls?" the travelers asked.

"The tolls?" Matt had completely forgotten his job. For the first time in his life he was enjoying his own birthday party and he didn't want anything to spoil it. "Forget the tolls. Enjoy yourselves," he cried. Matt looked at the young man. He was amazed at how lavish this man had been toward him. No one had ever treated him to a party—with balloons and streamers, no less! He didn't want the party to end.

The young man smiled warmly. "Great party isn't it? You ought to throw a few parties yourself! Why stop a good thing, right?"

"Right!" Matt laughed. "Why stop a good thing?"

"Oh, I know!" the man said, "Why not join us? You could be in charge of throwing parties and inviting others who have never been to any. Wouldn't that be great?"

Matt's eyes filled with tears. "I'd love it!"

"Good! Come and follow us! Oh, I almost forgot...my name is Jesus. Welcome, welcome to our party."

Matt belonged.

REFLECTION

As children, some of us were forced to become adults before we were ready. Our playful, childlike side was suppressed in favor of the serious, adult side. The reasons why many adults shouldered adult burdens as children are many. In some cases, children had to parent a chemically-dependent adult. In other cases, they became surrogate spouses for a parent whose real partner was no longer physically or emotionally available. And some parents emphasized work so highly that there was no time for play.

Work was Matt's parents' priority and so it became his. There was no time for celebration, not even on birthdays or holidays. But celebration is essential to growth. There are times in our lives when we need the playful celebration of our light. Celebrations make us more aware of the gifts our lives are to ourselves and to others. We all need to shine, and celebrations afford those opportunities. Without celebrations during which we can admire another's light, or be admired, shame can flourish. "I am inadequate and inferior" is the feeling response to a light never celebrated.

That shame can be so painful that our work becomes a compensation for our sense of the inadequacy of our own light. By throwing ourselves into our work we try to razzle dazzle others and ourselves into believing we are adequate. And we can never stop this razzle dazzle because we fear there'll be only darkness once the show of light is over.

From time to time all of us need to re-evaluate the place of work in our lives. For some of us, this stepping back is the first step forward. Only then can we realize our light isn't shining because of what we *do*, but because of who we *are*! Is that the step we need to take?

IN PRAISE OF OURSELVES

"The reign of God is like the case of the owner of an estate who went out at dawn to hire workmen for his vineyard. After reaching an agreement with them for the usual daily wage, he sent them out to his vineyard." Matthew 20:1-16

"Two hundred bucks for a day's work! That's fantastic!" Bert marveled.

"Oh! Oh! We don't deserve it! We don't deserve it!" Elmer wept with joy. "What a boss! What can I say about him? I'm at a loss. I am at a loss. He's..."

"Beyond compare," Bert bellowed.

"A man of vision," Elmer prophesied.

"The best in my book," Bert tapped his chest.

"A man for all seasons!" Elmer extended his arms. Neither Elmer nor Bert had been employed for a month and they were almost broke. The owner of *The Bottom's Up* winery had come to their rescue by hiring them. "And wait 'til the fellas in the other vineyards hear what we're being paid! They'll be green with envy." Elmer rubbed his hands with glee.

"Yeah," Bert chuckled. "I can hear them now. 'How do you guys rate? What's your secret?' I'll tell them that we don't rate. We've got no secret. We're not special. It just happened this way. The boss saw us and liked us!"

"'Liked us.' Be sure and add that," Elmer cautioned. "We don't want to make it look like we had nothing going for us, now do we?"

"You have a point," Bert said. "We wouldn't want them thinking that the boss was into his own hootch when he chose us to work. Speaking of work, we'd better stop our gabbing and earn our keep." So the two day laborers picked grapes alongside the regular workers. At noon they stopped for lunch.

Sitting in the shade offered by the leafy oaks, they noticed about eight old men coming through the gates. Dressed in threadbare, oversized suit coats and baggy pants, they looked like they hadn't shaved for two or three days. Shuffling into the vineyard, some of them held beer cans in one hand while supporting one another with the other.

"What's this? What's this?" Bert muttered. "Look what we're getting now! A bunch of old drunks. I wonder where the boss got them? Probably hiding in some bar, drinking up their welfare checks! I know those kind. The boss has saddled himself with some real losers. I hope he gives them what they deserve. Lucky he's got us."

"Yeah," Elmer agreed. "You don't find our kind in bars or cheap motels. I bet he's singing *our* praises after picking up *those* guys. Let's go back to work. I can't stomach watching their kind come in for a free ride." And back to work they went.

Around midafternoon they took a break. Munching an apple, Bert's eyes widened as he saw four or five men and women hobble through the gate on crutches, while three or four others who were blind tapped their canes as they inched along. They were followed by a few paraplegics who wheeled their way toward the vines. "Do you see what I see?" he cried. "This is incredible! He's hired a whole hospital ward of cripples. I wonder if he knows what he's doing. I hate to say it, but..." he whispered, "I think the boss is a little balmy."

"Out to lunch," Elmer whispered back.

"And dinner," Bert sniggered. "The boss can thank God he's got us! We're keeping this place going. I bet he's singing alleluias and offering incense because he met up with us. Two hundred bucks is a small price to pay for the likes of us. Right?"

"Roger," Elmer said. Saluting each other, they scanned the vineyard that the boss had gratefully entrusted to them. Then they went back to work.

It was late afternoon when Bert happened to look in the direction of the gate. "No!" he gasped. "It can't be! Elmer, Elmer! Look!" This time about nine laughing children ran, skipped, and cartwheeled through the gate. Clapping and dancing on the field, they then tugged the vines. "Kids don't know the first thing about work," Bert snapped. "All they can do is play."

"Now I *know* the boss is daffy," Elmer said. "No business sense! Doesn't understand that we all have to get money the old fashioned way—we have to earn it! I'm surprised he hasn't gone under. Well, I guess he can thank people like us for the fact that he stays afloat. There but for the grace of us goes he. He's indebted to us! He doesn't deserve us!"

"We're beyond compare!"

"The best in our books!"

"Men for all seasons!"

"What a paycheck we'll be getting," they sang as they danced in a little circle and then continued working.

When the workday ended, Elmer and Bert rushed to the pay office and stood first in line, pushing aside all others.

"He'll want to see us first," Bert said.

"Undoubtedly," Elmer agreed.

But a voice over the loudspeaker indicated otherwise. "Workers who were hired late this afternoon please come to the beginning of the line and those hired early this morning go to the end!"

"Wha..." Bert's mouth dropped open. "What's happening?"

"I guess when everybody else has left," Elmer confided, "the boss will be throwing a big party in our honor. And he certainly doesn't want them hangin' around. They don't deserve it."

"Yeah, that must be it," Bert said.

After they had gone to the end of the line, the voice over the loudspeaker continued. "Now I'll begin giving two hundred dollars to each of the workers. Please step forward!"

"They're getting two hundred bucks and they've only worked an hour!" Bert blurted. "Those kids are getting two hundred bucks! For doing nothing!"

"Don't worry," Elmer said as he wiped the perspiration gathering on his forehead. "Can you imagine what he's going to give us? I know it won't be what we're worth, but you can be sure we'll be able to live very comfortably. Wait and see!"

When they reached the office, an elderly gentleman sitting at a desk smiled and handed each of them two hundred dollars. Bert and Elmer looked at the money, then at one another, and then at the boss. "This is it?" they asked.

"Yes," the old man said.

"But, but..." Bert stammered, "we're worth more. You, you owe us much more."

"Yes," Elmer added. "We let you hire us. Is this how you thank us?"

"I beg your pardon," the old man said as he cupped his hand to his ear. "Am I hearing you right? You *let* me hire *you*? I ought to thank you?"

Ignoring his questions, Elmer pressed on. "We deserve more than two hundred bucks, much more. You're indebted to us."

The man laughed. "I'm indebted to *you*? Ha! Ha!" Scrutinizing their faces, he said, "I thought I recognized you boys. Every time you're down to your last cent I hire you. You sing my praises for an hour, and then your own the rest of the day. Don't you?"

"Why, I'm..." Bert scratched his head.

"You can't accept the fact that I like to help people because I get a kick out of it, can you? I do it not because people are so darned good that I *have* to pay them but because I *enjoy* paying them!" The old man shook his head sadly.

Embarrassed, Bert and Elmer stood silently with their heads lowered. They were ready to walk out of the office when the old man raised a hand and said, "Wait! I suppose you expected me to throw a party for you, too, didn't you?" More silence. Winking, he said, "Well, you're not going to get the bash you probably expected but we can go into the back room and share a cup of wine and some cheese and crackers. You think you fellas can settle for something 'less' than you deserve?" he laughed.

Bert and Elmer swallowed hard, nodded and followed the old man. For the moment, they were grateful they had something to eat.

REFLECTION

Talk to physicians or lawyers or clergy or social workers: They'll tell you. Clients are desperate for their help before they've given their services. "We need you. Tell us what to do," they implore. They're mighty grateful and willing to pay whatever is necessary to get well or settle some legal dispute or get some kind of intervention in a marital or family dispute. But once the crisis is over, well, that is a different matter.

"I could have done it myself," they say, or "Why do I have to pay you so much money for the operation or the counseling or the legal fees? You people owe us a lot. If it weren't for us, you'd be out of business!" The predictable course of events for many clients is from deep indebtedness to contempt for services rendered. Why?

As in our story, people conveniently forget what they have

received and then they rationalize their lack of gratitude by attacking the very people who helped them. "We deserve what you did for us," is the assumption. Deserving all too often cancels out gratitude. The trees, the birds, the air, people—they are all there for us. We deserve them!

But we not only take others for granted; we take ourselves for granted as well. In other words, we no longer rejoice in our own light. But a light taken for granted might just as well be hidden under a basket, because it is no longer noticed. Remembering is essential in being grateful, and gratitude helps us be aware of the gift that each light is.

Do we appreciate the gifts of light shining in our presence? Or have we forced them in hiding by taking them for granted? Are we no longer even aware of them?

TALENTS

"The case of a man who was going on a journey is similar. He called in his servants and handed his funds over to them according to each man's abilities. To one he disbursed five thousand silver pieces, to a second two thousand, and to a third a thousand."

Matthew 25:14-15

"Hi!" Louie smiled and waved at people in expensive cars, beat-up jalopies, taxis, school buses, eighteen-wheelers, and pickup trucks. It didn't matter whether the passersby were seniors, teenagers, schoolchildren, or hefty truck drivers. Louie had been greeting people on his street corner every day for forty years. That is all he did!

When he first started, people called him screwy Louie. "Why's he doing that? What's he smiling for? Who's he saying 'hi' to?" they asked as they craned their necks for a better view.

"You're mental! They ought to lock you up," were the cruelest comments a few ignorant people hurled at him as they sped by his corner. Gradually, though, those who regularly drove past Louie began to anticipate his familiar greeting. Sometimes a husband and wife who had been arguing called a truce just long enough to wave and comment on Louie's greeting. Chubby-cheeked boys and giggling girls waved wildly on their way to school in yellow buses. Occasionally a matronly woman stopped her car and handed Louie a box of chocolate chip cookies.

Yes, Louie had been saying "hi" for forty-four years. Brain-damaged as a baby when he fell out of a crib, he had spent his childhood playing quietly with his toys. And when he became a teenager he did nothing else but rock away his time and look at pictures in comic books. Louie's parents had long ago despaired of Louie doing anything constructive. "Let's face it," his dad harped whenever the subject came up, "Louie has no future. He'll be looking at comic books forever."

Louie's parents were grateful they had at least one son who showed real promise. Lenny, their youngest, had brains and good looks. "I'm gonna be a lawyer. You wait and see," he promised his folks.

"Our son's going to be a lawyer. Just wait and see," they bragged to relatives, neighbors, to anyone who cared to listen. There wasn't much they could say about Louie, and they felt embarrassed describing his preoccupation with comic books. Nor were they interested in discussing their middle son, Larry. "We hope he grows up some day. All he does is sit around, talk for hours on the phone to his girlfriends, and raid the refrigerator," they sighed. "Oh, yeah," they added as an afterthought, "Larry likes to go into Louie's room, wave, and say 'hi' to him." Then they'd laugh. "He thinks Louie is actually going to answer him some day. What a pair of losers!"

One day when Larry was bounding past Louie's room, he leaned in, smiling and waving and, as usual, cheerily bellowed "hi." Then, as he turned to leave, he thought he heard a quiet "hi" come back to him. Wheeling back, Larry cried, "Louie, you said 'hi'!"

This time Louie smiled, waved, and said more loudly than before, "Hi!" Larry was beside himself. He dashed over to Louie, hugged him, ran out of the room, and told his folks. They were pleased but certainly not elated.

"Isn't that nice," they agreed. "Our son can say 'hi' at last.

Let's hope he can learn more—complete sentences." They were happy for him, but a wave, a smile, and a "hi" didn't come close to what their son Lenny would accomplish one day when he became a lawyer. Larry, on the other hand, marveled over Louie's accomplishment and his role in getting Louie to respond. He decided then and there to make a career out of helping people with problems similar to Louie's.

"Well, of course, it's better than doing nothing," his folks conceded when Larry told them what he intended to do. And, in the privacy of their bedroom they observed, "He'll never succeed like Lenny but there isn't anything we can do about that."

Lenny had the brains and the looks, all right. He also had the gift of gab. "I'm gonna be a lawyer. You just wait and see!" And everybody waited. Louie, on the other hand, wasted little time using his newfound talent. He took his next big step when he put his comic books on a shelf, walked to the front door, opened it, and stepped out onto the porch. There he waved at letter carriers, kids delivering papers, bill collectors, neighbors. He made them all feel welcome. Pleased with his success, he finally strode proudly to the corner of his block where a new world eagerly waited his presence, his talent.

And among the many persons who waved every day to Louie was Larry as he drove to the hospital where he worked as a physical therapist for children.

As for Lenny, if anyone cared to look closely enough, on any afternoon he could be seen muttering from a swing on his porch, "I'm gonna be a lawyer some day. You just wait and see!"

REFLECTION

Lights don't need to be floodlights in order to illumine.
Children need parents who facilitate the emergence of even
the smallest light in their children. Parents who either discou-
rage their children from shining, or who expect them to be the
whole stellar system, produce similar results: Their children's
light remains hidden.

This story illustrates what happens when a child's feeble
light is not appropriately recognized or mirrored by parents.
Since the child's sense of self depends on affirmation, a failure
to notice means the child experiences a deficient self. Thus,
Louie sits in his rocker day in and day out. What little he had
to offer was never affirmed until his brother Larry consistent-
ly acknowledged him.

Expecting too much, however, also places too much of a
burden on a child. When we brag about our children's gifts,
we want to bear in mind that affirming their achievements
isn't the same as imposing unattainable goals on them. This
generates anxiety instead of self-confidence. None of us ought
to have to bear the burden of being the best of anything. It is
enough that we be who we are. In being that, we discover
what kind of light we really are and not just what kind of light
our parents had intended. Lenny's failure is that no one was
around to affirm him in his limitations as well as in his suc-
cesses. "You don't need to be perfect and that is fine," is the
message that he needed to hear and didn't.

But what Louie heard from Larry sustained him, and the
first steps he took, though small, were his first steps out from
under the basket. Once he was out, Louie's flickering match-
light became a beacon of light to all the travelers who passed
his way. Can we recognize that very small steps are very important ones in coming out from under the basket?

WHO'S LOST?

"Who among you, if he has a hundred sheep and loses one of them, does not leave the ninety-nine in the wasteland and follow the lost one until he finds it?" Luke 15:4

He returned to the house with them and again the crowd assembled, making it impossible for them to get any food whatever. When his family heard of this they came to take charge of him, saying, "He is out of his mind." Mark 3:20

"Every family has one!"
"And he's ours..."
"Without a doubt!"
"The black sheep!"
The black sheep? Who were Jesus' cousins talking about as they sat fanning themselves on the porch that hot afternoon in Nazareth?
"Yes, Jesus is our black sheep," Joe nodded gravely. "He doesn't take after his mom or his dad. I don't know of any of us who are as crazy as he is. I'd say John comes the closest. He's really weird—eating insects, into leather, and a real hellraiser with the authorities!"
"But that's Mary's side of the family, not ours. I'm worried what people will think about us," Jim said.

"Right!" Joe waved a hand. "I've already had total strangers come up to me and say, 'You're Jesus' cousin, aren't you? What's he up to anyway?' What can I say? What can any of us say? That he's running around the countryside giving pep talks to losers about some pie-in-the-sky day when they'll all be winners?"

"Or that he wastes time telling stories and hanging out with guys who are out of work like himself," Jim added. "And if that isn't enough, that Jesus parties with pretty shady characters, doesn't have a place of his own, and wears the same outfit his mom gave him two years ago!"

"Yeah, I know he got a kick out of the fact that it's a one-piece tunic, but enough is enough already!" Joe shook his head. "What bothers me most are the wild stories I'm beginning to hear about him acting like some faith healer: laying hands on the crazies and trying to touch others' hurts away."

"You'd think he was some heaven-sent masseur!" Jim interrupted, his voice tinged with sarcasm. "Let me tell you, these stories worry me, too, but not half as much as the reports I'm getting about his run-ins with the authorities. Seems he doesn't like the way they keep shop. He scolds them for preferring their pocketbooks to the poor; chastises them for endlessly primping and preening in public; and lashes out at them for saddling those he calls 'the little ones' with oppressive laws. I tell you, if he keeps undermining their authority, you, I, and the whole family are in for trouble," Jim concluded ominously.

"Yes, they'll send a team down here to snoop around and dig up dirt to implicate all of us with trumped up charges," Joe warned. "We've got to do something before that happens. We've got to go to Capernaum where they say he's hanging out and bring him back with us."

"I'm not certain he'll listen to us," Jim said. "I don't think he trusts us. But if we can get Mary to come, he may give us a hearing. She hasn't seen him for a while and we'll tell her we'd like to visit Jesus and we'd like her to join us."

"Good idea," Joe said. "Remember, no talk about him being a problem child. She thinks the world of him—like he's God's gift to the world and all that. While we're walking, we'll just try to convince her that maybe Jesus needs a little rest and we'd like him to come home for a while. She'd like that. Maybe she'd even make him a new tunic!"

"Yeah, might even get him to cut his hair and shave!" Jim said.

"Now you're talking! Well let's get at it! We can't lose any time," Joe said.

Jim and Joe persuaded Mary to come along with them to Capernaum. She seemed puzzled by their sudden solicitude for Jesus, since they had never seemed fond of him when he lived at home. As Mary remembered it, Jesus had often tried to be their friend, but they always had excuses for not spending time with him. Even at family get-togethers Jim and Joe avoided Jesus. But then those two tended to go their own ways, avoiding most of the other family members as well. "I wish I could reach them," Jesus had told his folks on several occasions. However, now the two wanted to visit Jesus, and even though Mary had reservations about their intentions, she decided to give them the benefit of the doubt.

They arrived at the public square in Capernaum just in time to see a large crowd gathered around a man who was speaking to them. Joe shaded his eyes from the noonday sun, squinted, and cried, "It's Jesus!" The three walked as quickly as possible to the gathering. As they stood at the back of the crowd, Mary tapped her finger on a big, burly man's shoulder. After she had gotten his attention she told him she was Jesus' mother and asked if he could muscle his way through the crowd to tell Jesus she and his cousins were waiting to see him. The man grumbled, hesitated, but finally angled his way through the crowd and disappeared.

A couple of minutes later he returned. Laughing, he told her, "Jesus says we're all his relatives if we act like family and care for one another the way God wants us to do."

"Now what's that supposed to mean?" Joe asked angrily.

"Hey, buddy, I'm just giving you the message. Interpret it any way you like. If you're his cousin, you oughta know what he's talking about. You've always cared about him, haven't you?"

"Of course, I..." Joe was going to say he had always cared but he noticed Mary's eyes fixed on him and he said nothing more.

Pressing the point, the man directed his comments to Jim, "I mean you'd try to reach out to him if you thought he was in trouble. Right?"

"Well, I..." He, too, caught Mary's eye and sputtered, "I ...I...I...of course, of course!" By this time the crowd had thinned out and the two men took advantage of the situation.

Joe elbowed Jim. "Let's get away from this guy! He's getting to me." They practically carried Mary as they shoved their way to the center of the crowd. "He's telling a story," Joe whispered.

"Who among you, if he has a hundred sheep and loses one of them, does not leave the ninety-nine in the wasteland and follow the lost one until he finds it? And when he finds it, he puts it on his shoulders in jubilation. Once arrived home, he invites friends and neighbors in and says to them, 'Rejoice with me because I have found my lost sheep.' I tell you, there will likewise be more joy in heaven over one repentant sinner than over ninety-nine righteous people who have no need to repent." After Jesus had finished, his face lit up as he caught sight of Mary and his cousins. "Mom," he cried as he ran over to her and gave her a big hug. "Jim, Joe, what a surprise! I was just thinking about you. I've found you at last!"

"Thinking about us?" Joe puzzled.

"Found us?" Jim muttered. "Why..." Jim couldn't finish the sentence since Jesus was embracing them both like long lost brothers.

"You're going to stay for a while, aren't you?"

"Well..." The brothers looked sheepishly at one another. "We...uh..."

"Of course you are. We've got so much to talk about. And nothing is more important than being with you...and Mom, of course," Jesus laughed.

Tears formed in the eyes of the two brothers as they put their arms around Jesus' waist. They had come to bring the black sheep home with them and for some strange reason they felt they were being welcomed back into the fold...where they belonged.

REFLECTION

"I'm lost! I hope I can find my way," could as easily be the cry of someone who finds no meaning in life as it could be the complaint of a frustrated driver in a strange city. Yet the simple admission that we are lost is essential if we are ever to find our way. Unfortunately, we do not make these admissions easily. Just as we can insist that we know where we're going as we drive around in circles in the strange city, so we can also insist that we know where we're going in life when we really don't. Mindlessly watching television, endlessly having affairs, or working nonstop day after day are a few of the ways in which we get lost and lose all sense of purpose and meaning in life.

However, once we recognize that we are at a loss about what to do with our lives, then we are already beginning to walk in the light. No one is as far gone as the one who is completely unaware of being lost. Rather than despairing of finding our way once we have seen the light and admitted to being lost, we might regard that very insight, intuition, or recognition as a first step in coming out from under the basket.

How do we react when we discover we have been lost? Do we despair or become depressed? Or do we see that "seeing" is itself light, a gift from the Light?

LECTIONARY REFERENCES

Line Drawing	Luke 10:25 ff: 15th Sunday in Ordinary Time, C Cycle
Last Laugh	Genesis 18:1 ff: 16th Sunday in Ordinary Time, C Cycle
Who's Deserving?	Jonah 3:1 ff: 3rd Sunday in Ordinary Time, B Cycle; Monday of the 27th Week in Ordinary Time, Year 1
Short on Memory	Matthew 18:21 ff: 24th Sunday in Ordinary Time, A Cycle; Tuesday of the 3rd Week in Lent, Years 1, 2
Risen	Matthew 13:33 ff: 16th Sunday in Ordinary Time, A Cycle; Monday of the 17th Week in Ordinary Time, Years 1, 2
Pearlie	Matthew 13:45 ff: 17th Sunday in Ordinary Time, A Cycle; Wednesday of the 17th Week in Ordinary Time, Years 1, 2
The Treasure	Matthew 13:44 ff: 17th Sunday in Ordinary Time, A Cycle; Wednesday of the 17th Week in Ordinary Time, Years 1, 2
A Fish Story	Matthew 13:47 ff: 17th Sunday in Ordinary Time, A Cycle; Thursday of the 17th Week in Ordinary Time, Years 1, 2
The Chocolate Man	Luke 16:1 ff: 25th Sunday in Ordinary Time, C Cycle; Friday of the 31st Week in Ordinary Time, Years 1, 2

Giveaway	Luke 16:1 ff: 25th Sunday in Ordinary Time, C Cycle; Friday of the 31st Week in Ordinary Time, Years 1, 2
Joanna	Luke 14:25 ff: 23rd Sunday in Ordinary Time, C Cycle; Wednesday of the 31st Week, Years 1, 2
Going Places	Luke 14:11 ff: 22nd Sunday in Ordinary Time, C Cycle; Saturday of the 30th Week, Years 1, 2
New World	Luke 10:40 ff: 16th Sunday in Ordinary Time, C Cycle; Wednesday of the 27th Week, Years 1, 2
Our Kind	Mark 5:1 ff: Monday of the 4th Week, Years 1, 2
Broken Promise	Luke 24:13 ff: Easter Sunday, ABC; 3rd Sunday of Easter, A Cycle; Wednesday of the Octave of Easter, Years 1, 2
The Topbanana Tree	Genesis 3:1 ff: Friday of the 5th Week in Ordinary Time, Year 1
Narrow Door	Luke 13:22 ff: 21st Sunday in Ordinary Time, C Cycle; Wednesday of the 30th Week in Ordinary Time, Years 1, 2
Daddy	Luke 15:11 ff: 4th Sunday in Lent, C Cycle; Saturday of the 2nd Week of Lent, Years 1, 2
The Party	Matthew 9:9 ff: 10th Sunday in Ordinary Time, A Cycle; feast of St. Matthew, Sept. 21; Friday of the 13th Week, Years 1, 2

In Praise of Ourselves   Matthew 20:1 ff: 25th Sunday in Ordinary
                             Time, A Cycle

Talents   Matthew 25:14 ff: Saturday of the 21st
                             Week in Ordinary Time, Years 1, 2

Who's Lost?   Mark 3:20 ff: 10th Sunday in Ordinary
                             Time, B Cycle; Saturday of the 2nd Week in
                             Ordinary Time, Years 1, 2